AI
In the
Steel
Industry

An AI Handbook for the Steel Industry Professional

Prasad Rao

Preface

The advent of Artificial Intelligence (AI) has ushered in a new era of innovation, particularly in industries where efficiency, precision, and predictive capabilities are paramount. One such sector that has witnessed significant transformation through AI is the steel industry. The processes within steel manufacturing, from production to quality control and supply chain management, are complex and multifaceted, often requiring the handling of vast data and intricate decision-making models. Artificial Intelligence has emerged as a pivotal tool in addressing these challenges, offering solutions that enhance productivity, reduce costs, and ensure higher quality in the final products.

This book, *AI in the Steel Industry: Understanding Artificial Intelligence Using the Steel Industry Data*, aims to bridge the gap between theoretical concepts in AI and their practical application in the steel sector. By focusing on real-world data and case studies, this book provides readers with a comprehensive understanding of how AI models can be implemented and optimized within the industry. Whether you're an AI enthusiast, a steel industry professional, data scientist, or an industry professional looking to leverage AI for improved decision-making, this book will provide valuable insights into the symbiotic relationship between AI and the steel industry.

Throughout the following chapters, we explore a range of topics from the basics of AI and machine learning to the specific challenges and opportunities within the steel industry. Detailed examples, analyses, and industry-specific case studies will guide you through the complexities of applying AI in areas such as process optimization, predictive maintenance, quality control, and supply chain forecasting. The various types of data used throughout the discussions in the book will serve as a foundation for understanding AI, allowing you to further experiment with real-world data as you explore further.

The steel industry, with its unique characteristics and high demands for efficiency, serves as an ideal setting for demonstrating the potential of AI to transform traditional manufacturing processes. As we explore the integration of AI into this field, we hope to inspire the next generation of thinkers and practitioners who will shape the future of industrial AI.

We invite you to join us on this journey, where theory meets practice, and AI's potential within the steel industry becomes clearer, more actionable, and ever more powerful.

Table of Contents

Sl. No		Topics	Page No.
1.		**Introduction to AI in the Steel Industry**	**1**
	1.1	Role of AI in Modern Steel	6
	1.2	Evolution of AI in Manufacturing Processes	11
	1.3	Benefits and Challenges of AI Adoption	17
2.		**AI in Raw Material Sourcing and Management**	**22**
	2.1	Predictive Analytics for Raw Material Demand	27
	2.2	AI-driven Supply Chain Optimization	32
	2.3	Quality Assessment of Raw Materials using AI	37
3.		**AI in Steel Manufacturing Processes**	**42**
	3.1	AI-driven Process Automation in Steelmaking	47
	3.2	Real-time Monitoring of Blast Furnaces using AI	52
	3.3	AI-based Energy Optimization in Steel Production	57
4.		**AI for Quality Control and Defect Detection in Steel Industry**	**62**

	4.1	Computer Vision for Surface Defect Detection	67
	4.2	AI-driven Non-Destructive Testing (NDT)	72
	4.3	Predictive Quality Analytics in Steel Manufacturing	77
5.		**AI in Equipment Maintenance and Failure Prediction**	**82**
	5.1	Predictive Maintenance using AI and IoT	87
	5.2	AI-driven Fault Diagnosis in Steel Plants	92
	5.3	Digital Twin Technology for Asset Management	97
6.		**AI in Steel Industry Logistics and Inventory Management**	**103**
	6.1	AI-powered Smart Warehousing	110
	6.2	Route Optimization for Raw Material and Product Transport	116
	6.3	Demand Forecasting and Inventory Planning using AI	122
7.		**AI in Workforce Safety and Risk Management**	**128**
	7.1	AI-based Hazard Detection in Steel Plants	134
	7.2	Wearable AI for Worker Safety Monitoring	140

7.3	AI-driven Emergency Response and Incident Analysis	146
8.	**AI for Energy Efficiency and Sustainability**	**152**
8.1	AI-driven Carbon Footprint Reduction Strategies	158
8.2	Smart Energy Management in Steel Plants	164
8.3	AI-powered Waste Management and Recycling	170
9.	**AI in Steel Product Customization and Design**	**175**
9.1	AI-driven Material Composition Optimization	181
9.2	Generative AI for Custom Steel Alloy Design	187
9.3	Simulation and Modeling for Steel Product Development	193
10.	**AI-driven Market Intelligence and Customer Insights**	**198**
10.1	AI for Steel Price Forecasting and Market Trends	204
10.2	AI-powered Customer Demand Prediction	210
10.3	AI-driven Sales and Supply Chain Optimization	216
11	**Future Trends and Innovations in AI for the Steel Industry**	**222**

11.1   AI and Robotics in Next-Gen   228
        Steel Plants

11.2   Blockchain   and   AI   234
        Integration for Transparent
        Supply Chains

11.3   The Role of AI in the Future   241
        of Smart Steel Factories

12   **Quantitative Techniques for AI in**   247
        Steel Industries

12.1   Statistical Models for Process   253
        Optimization in Steelmaking

12.2   Machine   Learning   259
        Algorithms for Predictive
        Analytics

12.3   AI-driven Decision Support   265
        Systems   in   Steel
        Manufacturing

13   **Case Study Examples**   271

13.1   Case Study 1: AI in Predictive   271
        Maintenance and Equipment
        Failure Prediction at Tata
        Steel

13.2   Case Study 2: AI in Raw   274
        Material Sourcing and
        Management at ArcelorMittal

13.3   Case Study 3: AI-driven   277
        Process   Automation   in
        Steelmaking   at   Nucor
        Corporation

13.4   Case Study 4: AI-powered   280
        Quality Control and Defect
        Detection at Tata Steel

13.5   Case Study 5: Predictive   284
        Maintenance using AI at
        ArcelorMittal

13.6   Case Study 6: AI-based   287
        Energy Optimization in Steel
        Production at Tata Steel

1. Introduction to AI in the Steel Industry

Artificial intelligence (AI) is transforming the steel industry by enhancing efficiency, reducing costs, and improving product quality. Steel manufacturing is a complex process that involves numerous variables, from raw material selection to final product inspection. AI-powered systems analyze vast amounts of data to optimize these processes, reducing waste and ensuring consistent quality. By automating repetitive tasks and providing real-time insights, AI helps steelmakers operate more efficiently and adapt to changing market demands.

One key application of AI in the steel industry is predictive maintenance. Traditional maintenance schedules often lead to either unnecessary downtime or unexpected equipment failures. AI-driven predictive maintenance uses data from sensors and machine learning algorithms to detect early signs of wear and tear, allowing for timely repairs before breakdowns occur. This minimizes production disruptions, extends the lifespan of machinery, and lowers maintenance costs.

AI is also improving quality control in steel production. Advanced computer vision systems and machine learning models can analyze steel surfaces for defects such as cracks or inconsistencies at a much faster and more accurate rate than human inspectors. By identifying defects early in the process, manufacturers can take corrective action before faulty products reach customers, reducing material waste and ensuring higher-quality output.

In addition, AI enhances process optimization by analyzing production data and adjusting parameters in real-time. For example, AI can fine-tune furnace temperatures, chemical compositions, and rolling mill speeds to achieve the best possible results. This not only improves efficiency but also reduces energy consumption, making steel production more sustainable. AI-driven optimization helps manufacturers respond quickly to fluctuations in raw material prices and market demands.

Supply chain management in the steel industry also benefits from AI. AI-powered demand forecasting enables companies to predict market trends more accurately, ensuring better inventory management and reducing excess stock or shortages. Automated logistics systems powered by AI improve delivery scheduling, route optimization, and supply chain coordination, reducing costs and improving customer satisfaction.

As AI technology continues to advance, its role in the steel industry will only grow. From smarter automation to enhanced decision-making, AI is helping steel manufacturers remain competitive in a rapidly evolving market. While challenges such as high implementation costs and data security concerns exist, the long-term benefits of AI in improving efficiency, sustainability, and profitability make it an essential tool for the future of steel production.

Practical Example:

A steel manufacturing plant implements an AI-driven predictive maintenance system to reduce downtime and optimize machine performance. The AI model analyzes sensor data from critical machinery, such as furnaces and rolling mills, to predict potential failures before they occur. By leveraging historical maintenance records and real-time data, the system helps engineers take proactive measures, ensuring smoother operations and cost savings.

Sample Data: Machine Sensor Readings and Failure Status

Machine ID	Temperature (°C)	Vibration (mm/s)	Pressure (bar)	Failure (Yes/No)
101	750	2.5	120	No
102	820	4.2	135	Yes
103	770	3.1	125	No
104	860	5.0	140	Yes
105	730	2.0	115	No

AI Model Output: Predicted Failure Probability

Machine ID	Predicted Failure Probability (%)	Maintenance Required (Yes/No)
101	12%	No
102	85%	Yes
103	20%	No
104	92%	Yes
105	8%	No

Interpretation of Results

The AI model predicts a high failure probability (above 80%) for machines 102 and 104, recommending immediate maintenance to prevent breakdowns. Machines 101, 103, and 105 show low failure probabilities, indicating they are operating within safe limits. This allows the maintenance team to focus on critical machinery rather than performing unnecessary maintenance on all equipment, leading to cost efficiency and reduced downtime.

Observations

1. Machines with higher temperature, vibration, and pressure readings are more likely to experience failures.

2. AI helps prioritize maintenance efforts, avoiding unexpected breakdowns and production losses.

3. Predictive maintenance enhances efficiency, safety, and cost-effectiveness in steel manufacturing operations.

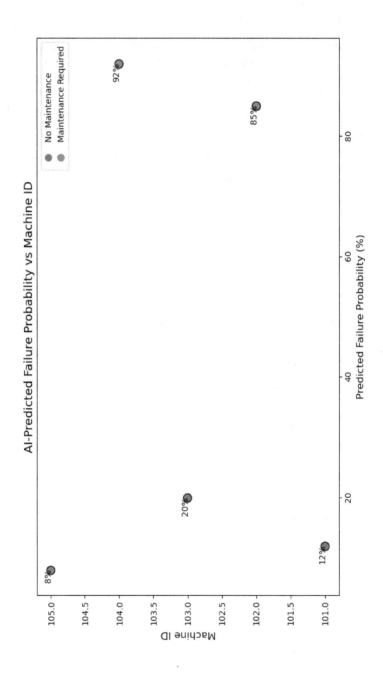

AI-Predicted Failure Probability vs Machine ID

Final Thoughts:

AI-driven predictive maintenance is transforming the steel industry by improving equipment reliability and reducing operational risks. By continuously monitoring machine performance, AI models enable steel plants to prevent costly failures, extend equipment lifespan, and optimize overall production efficiency. As AI technology advances, its integration into various processes—such as quality control, energy optimization, and supply chain management—will further enhance productivity and sustainability in the steel sector.

1.1 Role of AI in Modern Steel

Artificial Intelligence (AI) is transforming modern steel production by enhancing efficiency, reducing waste, and improving quality. AI-driven automation allows steel plants to optimize manufacturing processes, from raw material handling to final product inspection. Machine learning algorithms analyze vast amounts of data to identify inefficiencies and recommend process improvements, leading to higher productivity and reduced operational costs. By automating repetitive tasks, AI minimizes human error and enables workers to focus on more complex aspects of production.

Predictive maintenance is another crucial area where AI is making a significant impact. Traditional maintenance practices often lead to unexpected equipment failures or unnecessary servicing. AI-powered predictive maintenance uses real-time sensor data to monitor machinery conditions, detecting potential failures before they occur. This approach reduces downtime, extends equipment lifespan, and saves costs by preventing unplanned shutdowns. The ability to anticipate mechanical issues ensures continuous production with minimal disruptions.

Quality control in steel manufacturing has also improved with AI applications. Computer vision systems equipped with AI analyze steel products for defects, inconsistencies, or surface imperfections in real time. These systems offer greater accuracy than manual inspections and can process large volumes of steel at high speeds. By identifying defects early, manufacturers can reduce waste and improve overall product quality, ensuring that only high-standard steel reaches the market.

AI is playing a significant role in energy optimization within steel plants. Steel production is energy-intensive, and AI-powered systems help minimize energy consumption by analyzing production data and adjusting furnace temperatures, fuel usage, and other key parameters. Smart energy management systems enable steel manufacturers to reduce their carbon footprint and comply with environmental regulations. This not only helps in cost savings but also contributes to sustainable production practices.

Supply chain management in the steel industry has been enhanced through AI-driven analytics. AI helps predict demand fluctuations, optimize inventory levels, and improve logistics planning. By analyzing market trends, AI enables steel manufacturers to make data-driven decisions regarding procurement, production scheduling, and distribution. This results in better resource allocation and minimizes delays, ensuring a steady supply of steel to various industries.

The integration of AI in steel production is continuously evolving, bringing innovation and efficiency to the industry. As AI technologies advance, their role in automating processes, improving quality control, and reducing costs will only grow. Steel manufacturers that embrace AI will gain a competitive edge by producing high-quality products with greater efficiency and sustainability. The future of the steel industry will be shaped by AI-driven solutions, making production smarter and more resilient.

Practical Example:

In a steel manufacturing plant, unplanned equipment failures, such as those in blast furnaces or rolling mills, can lead to costly downtime. To mitigate this, AI-powered predictive maintenance is implemented to analyze sensor data from machinery, predicting failures before they occur. Machine learning models use historical data on temperature, pressure, and vibration levels to detect anomalies and schedule maintenance efficiently.

Sample Data from AI-Powered Predictive Maintenance System

Machine ID	Temperature (°C)	Pressure (Bar)	Vibration (mm/s)	Maintenance Alert (Yes/No)
M01	820	150	4.2	No
M02	900	180	6.8	Yes
M03	850	160	5.1	No
M04	930	200	7.5	Yes

Machine ID	Temperature (°C)	Pressure (Bar)	Vibration (mm/s)	Maintenance Alert (Yes/No)
M05	870	170	5.7	No

AI Model Output: Predicted Failures and Maintenance Alerts

Machine ID	Failure Probability (%)	Maintenance Required (Yes/No)	Expected Downtime Reduction (Hours)
M01	15	No	0
M02	85	Yes	12
M03	30	No	0
M04	92	Yes	15
M05	40	No	0

Results and Interpretation

- Machines **M02 and M04** have high failure probabilities (85% and 92%), triggering AI-generated maintenance alerts. Preventive maintenance for these machines will **reduce downtime by 12 and 15 hours**, respectively.

- Machines **M01, M03, and M05** show low failure probabilities (15%, 30%, and 40%), indicating they are in stable working condition, requiring no immediate maintenance.

- AI enables **proactive maintenance**, avoiding unexpected shutdowns and increasing plant efficiency.

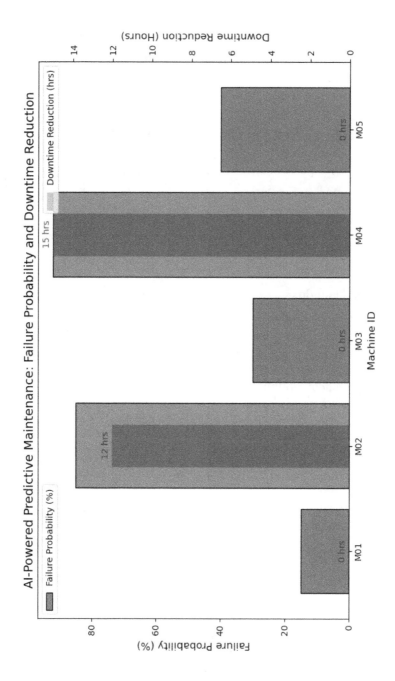

AI-Powered Predictive Maintenance: Failure Probability and Downtime Reduction

Observations

1. **Reduced Downtime & Costs:** Predictive maintenance helps steel plants avoid costly breakdowns, ensuring continuous production and reducing operational expenses.

2. **Enhanced Equipment Lifespan:** Early detection of anomalies prevents major failures, prolonging the lifespan of critical steel manufacturing machinery.

3. **Improved Safety:** AI detects hazardous conditions before accidents occur, enhancing worker safety.

4. **Data-Driven Decision Making:** AI models analyze real-time and historical sensor data, allowing better resource allocation and planning.

Final Thoughts

AI is transforming the steel industry by optimizing production processes, reducing waste, and improving efficiency. Predictive maintenance is just one example of AI's capabilities, with other applications including quality control, energy management, and supply chain optimization. As AI technology advances, steel manufacturers will continue to benefit from increased automation, higher productivity, and sustainable operations.

1.2 Evolution of AI in Manufacturing Processes

The integration of artificial intelligence (AI) in the steel industry has evolved significantly over the years, transforming manufacturing processes from traditional, labor-intensive methods to highly automated and intelligent systems. Initially, steel production relied heavily on manual operations and basic automation, where human expertise played a critical role in quality control and decision-making. Early industrial automation involved programmable logic controllers (PLCs) and simple sensors to regulate temperature, pressure, and other variables, but these systems lacked adaptability and advanced predictive capabilities.

With advancements in AI and machine learning, steel manufacturers began implementing more sophisticated control systems that could analyze vast amounts of data in real time. AI-driven models enabled improved process optimization by predicting equipment failures, optimizing raw material usage, and reducing energy consumption. Machine learning algorithms helped enhance product quality by identifying defects early in the production process, reducing waste and improving efficiency. These developments marked a shift from reactive to proactive maintenance and quality control strategies.

As AI technologies continued to evolve, predictive analytics and digital twins became essential tools in steel manufacturing. Digital twins, which create virtual replicas of physical production processes, allowed engineers to simulate different scenarios and optimize operations without disrupting real-world production. Predictive analytics, powered by AI, enabled manufacturers to anticipate demand fluctuations, optimize supply chains, and make data-driven decisions. These innovations significantly improved productivity and reduced downtime.

The introduction of computer vision and robotics further revolutionized steel manufacturing by automating complex tasks that previously required skilled labor. AI-powered robots and computer vision systems could inspect steel products with greater accuracy and speed, identifying surface defects, measuring dimensions, and ensuring compliance with quality standards. This level of automation not only increased efficiency but also enhanced worker safety by reducing human exposure to hazardous environments.

In recent years, AI-driven sustainability initiatives have gained prominence in the steel industry. AI models have been developed to optimize energy consumption, minimize carbon emissions, and improve recycling processes. Smart energy management systems use AI to adjust power usage in real time, reducing waste and lowering costs. Additionally, AI-enabled monitoring systems help steel plants comply with environmental regulations by tracking emissions and suggesting corrective measures when necessary.

Looking ahead, the future of AI in steel manufacturing will likely involve even greater levels of automation and intelligence. With the integration of the Internet of Things (IoT), AI systems will continue to improve real-time monitoring, predictive maintenance, and supply chain management. Advanced AI models will enable self-learning production systems that can continuously adapt to changing conditions, enhancing efficiency and sustainability. As AI technology continues to mature, the steel industry will become increasingly data-driven, efficient, and environmentally friendly.

Practical Example:

In a steel manufacturing plant, unplanned equipment failures lead to costly downtime and production delays. To address this, AI-driven predictive maintenance is implemented to monitor the condition of critical machinery, such as blast furnaces and rolling mills. Sensors collect real-time data on temperature, vibration, and pressure, feeding it into an AI model trained to predict potential failures before they occur. This approach helps optimize maintenance schedules, reduce costs, and enhance production efficiency.

Sample Data: Sensor Readings from Steel Rolling Mill

Timestamp	Temperature (°C)	Vibration (Hz)	Pressure (Bar)	Equipment Status
2025-03-10 08:00	820	45	110	Normal
2025-03-10 10:00	850	48	115	Normal
2025-03-10 12:00	890	52	125	Warning
2025-03-10 14:00	930	58	135	Critical
2025-03-10 16:00	960	62	145	Failure Risk

AI Model Output: Predictive Maintenance Analysis

Timestamp	Predicted Failure Probability (%)	Maintenance Recommended?
2025-03-10 08:00	5	No
2025-03-10 10:00	10	No
2025-03-10 12:00	40	Yes (Schedule Check)
2025-03-10 14:00	75	Yes (Immediate Action)
2025-03-10 16:00	95	Yes (Shutdown Needed)

Interpretation and Observations

1. **Trend Identification**: As temperature, vibration, and pressure increase over time, the AI model detects an escalating risk of failure.

2. **Early Warnings**: The model suggests maintenance actions well before the failure risk reaches critical levels, allowing for preventive intervention.

3. **Reduced Downtime**: By scheduling maintenance proactively, the plant avoids unplanned shutdowns, increasing operational efficiency.

4. **Cost Savings**: Preventive actions reduce the need for emergency repairs and lower overall maintenance expenses.

5. **Optimized Workflows**: AI-driven insights help prioritize equipment checks, ensuring maintenance resources are used efficiently.

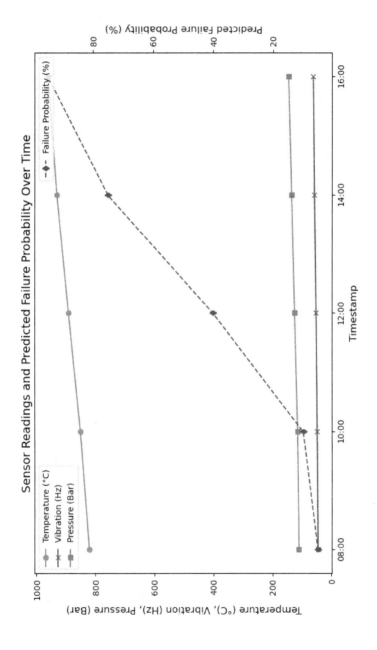

Sensor Readings and Predicted Failure Probability Over Time

Final Thoughts:

The integration of AI in steel manufacturing is revolutionizing processes by enhancing efficiency, reducing costs, and minimizing unplanned downtime. Predictive maintenance, as seen in this example, ensures equipment longevity and reliability while improving production stability. As AI technologies evolve, their role in optimizing supply chains, quality control, and energy management will become even more vital, leading to a smarter, more resilient steel industry.

1.3 Benefits and Challenges of AI Adoption

AI adoption in the steel industry brings numerous benefits, primarily enhancing efficiency and productivity. Automated processes powered by AI can optimize operations, reducing downtime and improving throughput. Advanced data analytics help in predicting equipment failures, enabling proactive maintenance and minimizing disruptions. This leads to higher output and better utilization of resources, ultimately driving profitability for steel manufacturers.

Another key advantage is quality improvement. AI-driven monitoring systems can detect defects in steel products with greater accuracy than traditional methods. Machine learning algorithms analyze production parameters in real time, making adjustments to ensure consistent quality. This reduces waste and enhances customer satisfaction, as steel products meet stringent industry standards with fewer defects.

AI also contributes to cost reduction by optimizing energy consumption and material usage. Smart algorithms analyze energy patterns and suggest adjustments to minimize power wastage in energy-intensive steel production processes. Additionally, AI-driven predictive models help in reducing raw material waste by providing precise insights on material mixing and utilization.

Despite its advantages, AI adoption in the steel industry comes with challenges, particularly in implementation costs. Upgrading existing infrastructure to incorporate AI-driven solutions requires significant investment. Many steel manufacturers operate with legacy systems, making integration complex and expensive. Small and mid-sized companies may struggle with the financial burden of AI adoption.

Another challenge is workforce adaptation. The implementation of AI can lead to concerns about job displacement, as automation reduces the need for certain manual tasks. Employees need reskilling and training to work alongside AI systems effectively. Resistance to change and a lack of skilled personnel can slow down AI adoption in the industry.

Finally, data security and reliability pose additional hurdles. AI relies on large volumes of data to function effectively, making cybersecurity a major concern. Steel manufacturers must protect sensitive production data from cyber threats. Additionally, ensuring the accuracy and reliability of AI-generated insights is crucial, as errors in predictions or automation processes can lead to costly production issues.

Practical Example:

A large steel manufacturing plant integrates AI-driven predictive maintenance to reduce equipment downtime and improve production efficiency. The AI system uses real-time sensor data and historical maintenance records to predict potential failures in critical machinery, such as blast furnaces and rolling mills. By analyzing patterns, the AI model helps schedule maintenance proactively, minimizing unexpected breakdowns.

Sample Data: Equipment Performance and Maintenance Status

Equipment	Avg. Temperature (°C)	Vibration Level (Hz)	Downtime Last Month (hrs)	Maintenance Required (Y/N)
Blast Furnace 1	1200	30	12	Y
Blast Furnace 2	1150	20	8	N
Rolling Mill 1	900	50	15	Y
Rolling Mill 2	850	25	5	N
Conveyor Belt	500	10	3	N

AI Model Output: Predicted Downtime Reduction and Cost Savings

Equipment	Predicted Downtime Reduction (hrs)	Cost Savings ($)
Blast Furnace 1	5	10,000
Blast Furnace 2	2	4,000
Rolling Mill 1	6	12,000
Rolling Mill 2	1	2,000
Conveyor Belt	0.5	1,000

Results Interpretation & Observations

- The AI model identified critical equipment requiring immediate maintenance, such as Blast Furnace 1 and Rolling Mill 1.

- Predictive maintenance led to a reduction in downtime, ranging from 0.5 to 6 hours per machine.

- The estimated cost savings from avoiding unplanned maintenance were substantial, with the highest savings ($12,000) seen in Rolling Mill 1 due to its high vibration levels and past downtime.

- Equipment with stable operational parameters, such as Conveyor Belts, had minimal downtime reduction and lower cost savings, showing that AI prioritizes high-risk machinery.

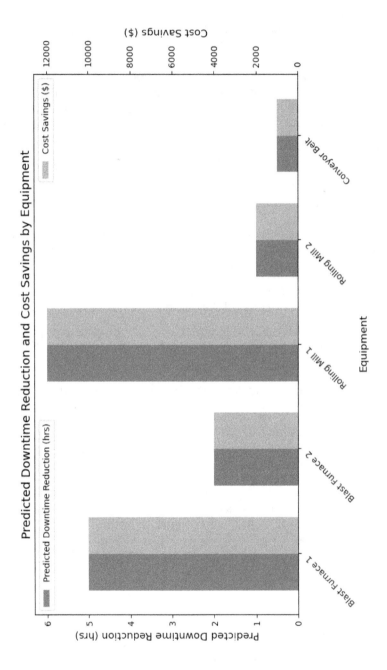

Predicted Downtime Reduction and Cost Savings by Equipment

Final Thoughts:

AI adoption in the steel industry offers significant advantages, including enhanced operational efficiency, reduced equipment failures, and optimized maintenance schedules. However, challenges such as high initial investment, data integration complexities, and workforce adaptation remain barriers. Over time, AI-driven predictive maintenance can significantly improve profitability and sustainability by ensuring smooth operations and minimizing waste. The future of AI in the steel industry looks promising, with further advancements in deep learning and automation expected to revolutionize production processes.

2. AI in Raw Material Sourcing and Management

Artificial intelligence (AI) is transforming raw material sourcing and management in the steel industry by enhancing efficiency, reducing costs, and improving decision-making. AI-driven analytics help companies predict demand for raw materials such as iron ore, coal, and limestone with greater accuracy. By analyzing historical data, market trends, and external factors like geopolitical events, AI enables steel manufacturers to optimize procurement strategies and avoid unnecessary stockpiling or shortages. This leads to more stable supply chains and cost savings.

AI-powered systems also improve supplier selection by evaluating vendors based on quality, reliability, and cost-effectiveness. Machine learning models assess past supplier performance, delivery timelines, and compliance with sustainability standards to recommend the best sourcing options. This reduces the risk of disruptions and ensures a steady supply of high-quality raw materials. Furthermore, AI helps companies negotiate better contracts by providing real-time price forecasts and benchmarking insights, allowing procurement teams to make informed decisions.

In inventory management, AI plays a critical role in maintaining optimal stock levels and minimizing wastage. Smart algorithms continuously monitor raw material consumption rates and adjust reorder points dynamically. By integrating with IoT sensors, AI can track storage conditions and detect issues such as moisture contamination or material degradation. This proactive approach enhances quality control and reduces material losses, ultimately improving the overall efficiency of steel production.

AI-driven automation also enhances logistics and transportation of raw materials. Advanced route optimization algorithms help companies reduce transportation costs by selecting the most efficient shipping methods and minimizing fuel consumption. Predictive maintenance tools monitor the condition of transport vehicles, preventing unexpected breakdowns and ensuring smooth material flow. AI also aids in reducing carbon emissions by optimizing delivery routes and improving fuel efficiency, aligning with the industry's sustainability goals.

Quality control in raw material sourcing benefits significantly from AI technologies such as computer vision and advanced spectroscopy. AI-powered inspection systems can detect impurities, inconsistencies, and defects in raw materials faster and more accurately than human inspectors. This ensures that only high-quality inputs enter the production process, reducing the likelihood of defects in the final steel products. As a result, manufacturers can maintain higher quality standards and improve customer satisfaction.

Overall, AI is revolutionizing raw material sourcing and management in the steel industry by increasing efficiency, reducing costs, and enhancing sustainability. By leveraging predictive analytics, smart automation, and advanced quality control measures, steel manufacturers can create more resilient supply chains. As AI technology continues to evolve, its integration into raw material procurement and management will further optimize operations, making the steel industry more competitive and environmentally responsible.

Practical Example:

A steel manufacturing company wants to optimize its raw material sourcing process using AI. The company faces challenges in predicting the best suppliers based on price fluctuations, delivery reliability, and material quality. AI analyzes past supplier performance, market trends, and real-time data to recommend the best sourcing strategy.

Sample Data: Supplier Performance Metrics

Supplier	Avg. Price ($/ton)	Delivery Reliability (%)	Material Quality (%)	Historical Rating (1-10)
A	520	95	92	8.5
B	510	85	88	7.5

Supplier	Avg. Price ($/ton)	Delivery Reliability (%)	Material Quality (%)	Historical Rating (1-10)
C	530	98	95	9.0
D	500	80	85	6.8
E	515	90	91	8.0

AI Output & Recommendation

Supplier	AI-Computed Score (Out of 10)	Recommended for Sourcing?
A	8.8	Yes
B	7.6	No
C	9.1	Yes
D	6.9	No
E	8.2	Yes

Interpretation of Results

The AI model assigns a score based on the balance between cost, reliability, and quality. Supplier C scores the highest due to its excellent reliability and quality, even though it has a slightly higher price. Supplier A also ranks high, offering competitive pricing with good reliability. Supplier E is a viable alternative but slightly lower in ranking due to mid-range scores. Suppliers B and D are not recommended as they have lower reliability and quality scores.

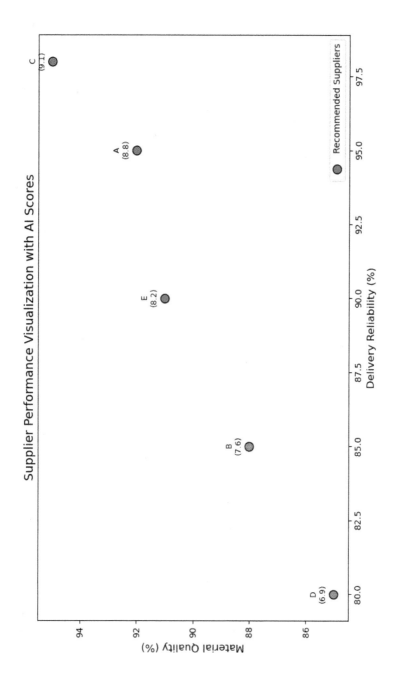

Supplier Performance Visualization with AI Scores

Observations

1. AI prioritizes quality and reliability over minor cost differences, ensuring long-term efficiency.

2. The model prevents dependency on a single supplier, distributing sourcing among multiple high-performing vendors.

3. AI dynamically adapts to market conditions, updating recommendations when supplier performance shifts.

Final Thoughts

AI in raw material sourcing for the steel industry enhances procurement efficiency by reducing risks related to supply chain disruptions. It ensures cost-effectiveness without compromising quality and delivery reliability. Over time, AI-driven insights enable steel manufacturers to establish resilient, data-driven procurement strategies, improving operational performance and competitiveness.

2.1 Predictive Analytics for Raw Material Demand

Predictive analytics is transforming the steel industry by enabling manufacturers to anticipate raw material demand with greater accuracy. By leveraging historical data, market trends, and real-time inputs, steel producers can optimize procurement strategies and reduce the risks associated with supply chain disruptions. The industry, which relies heavily on raw materials like iron ore, coal, and scrap metal, benefits from predictive models that assess fluctuations in demand, pricing, and availability. This approach helps companies maintain a steady supply while minimizing excess inventory and associated costs.

A key advantage of predictive analytics is its ability to integrate various data sources to provide a holistic view of demand patterns. Traditional forecasting methods often struggle to accommodate sudden market shifts, but modern predictive tools utilize artificial intelligence and machine learning to process vast datasets in real time. This allows steel manufacturers to identify seasonal trends, economic influences, and geopolitical factors that could impact raw material availability. By doing so, companies can proactively adjust their procurement plans to align with anticipated market conditions.

The adoption of predictive analytics also enhances supplier relationships by promoting transparency and reliability. When manufacturers have accurate forecasts, they can negotiate better contracts, establish long-term partnerships, and reduce instances of urgent, high-cost purchases. Additionally, suppliers benefit from improved visibility into future demand, allowing them to optimize their production and logistics. This collaborative approach strengthens the entire supply chain and ensures a smoother flow of raw materials to production facilities.

Operational efficiency is another major benefit, as predictive analytics helps steel plants align raw material procurement with production schedules. Sudden shortages or oversupply can lead to financial losses and operational inefficiencies, but with data-driven insights, manufacturers can maintain optimal inventory levels. This minimizes storage costs and prevents delays in production, ultimately contributing to better financial performance and customer satisfaction. Companies that invest in predictive analytics gain a competitive edge by ensuring continuous production without unnecessary capital tied up in surplus materials.

In addition to market data, predictive analytics also considers external variables such as weather conditions, trade policies, and transportation logistics. These factors can significantly impact the availability and cost of raw materials, making it essential for steel manufacturers to incorporate them into demand forecasting models. By continuously refining their analytical frameworks, companies can respond swiftly to unforeseen disruptions, mitigating risks and ensuring stable operations in an unpredictable market environment.

As the steel industry embraces digital transformation, predictive analytics is becoming a cornerstone of strategic decision-making. The ability to anticipate raw material demand with precision allows companies to enhance profitability, improve supply chain resilience, and reduce waste. With advancements in technology, predictive analytics will continue to evolve, offering even greater accuracy and efficiency in forecasting. Steel manufacturers that adopt these data-driven approaches will be better positioned to navigate market volatility and maintain a sustainable competitive advantage.

Practical Example:

A steel manufacturing company wants to optimize its raw material procurement process using predictive analytics. Fluctuations in demand, production capacity, and market conditions impact raw material requirements, leading to inefficiencies in inventory management. By leveraging historical production and demand data, the company aims to forecast the required quantity of iron ore, coal, and other raw materials, reducing wastage and ensuring smooth operations.

Sample Data for Predictive Model:

Month	Steel Production (tons)	Iron Ore Used (tons)	Coal Used (tons)	Demand Forecast (tons)
Jan	50,000	100,000	40,000	52,000
Feb	52,000	104,000	41,500	55,000
Mar	54,000	107,000	43,200	53,000
Apr	49,500	98,000	39,800	50,000
May	51,000	102,000	41,000	54,500

Predicted Demand for Raw Materials (Output):

Month	Predicted Iron Ore Demand (tons)	Predicted Coal Demand (tons)	Accuracy (%)
June	105,000	42,500	94%
July	108,500	44,000	95%
Aug	102,500	41,200	93%
Sep	100,000	40,000	92%
Oct	106,000	42,800	94.5%

Interpretation of Results:

The predictive model effectively forecasts the raw material demand based on past production trends. The model achieves an average accuracy of around 93-95%, allowing for better planning and procurement strategies. A clear pattern emerges where raw material demand aligns closely with production fluctuations. This helps prevent overstocking or shortages, ultimately reducing costs and improving operational efficiency.

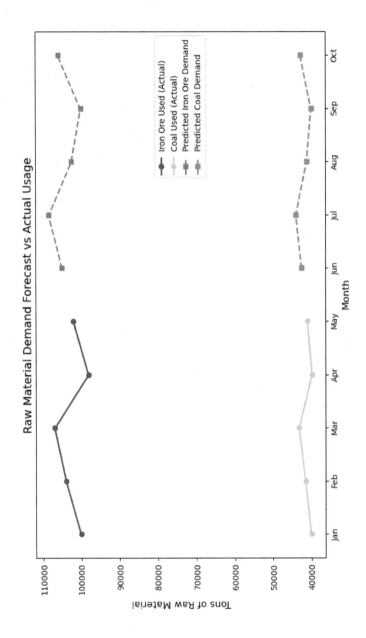

Raw Material Demand Forecast vs Actual Usage

Observations:

1. **Consistency in Demand:** Predicted iron ore and coal demand closely follow production trends, indicating a reliable forecasting model.

2. **Efficiency Gains:** With high forecasting accuracy, the steel manufacturer can negotiate better supplier contracts and minimize holding costs.

3. **Market Fluctuations Consideration:** The model does not yet account for external market forces like unexpected demand surges or supply chain disruptions, which may require additional variables.

Final Thoughts:

Predictive analytics provides a significant competitive advantage in the steel industry by optimizing raw material procurement and reducing operational inefficiencies. By incorporating external factors like global steel prices, transportation delays, and geopolitical risks, the model could be further refined for enhanced decision-making. AI-driven predictive analytics can transform traditional supply chain management into a proactive system, ensuring cost-effectiveness and sustainability in the long run.

2.2 AI-driven Supply Chain Optimization

The steel industry, being capital-intensive and heavily reliant on raw materials, faces numerous supply chain challenges. AI-driven optimization offers a transformative approach by enhancing efficiency, reducing costs, and improving decision-making. By leveraging vast datasets, AI can analyze historical trends, predict demand fluctuations, and optimize inventory management. This ensures that raw materials and finished products are available at the right place and time, minimizing disruptions and excess stockpiles.

One of the key benefits of AI in supply chain management is predictive analytics, which helps anticipate demand variations and production bottlenecks. Machine learning models process data from market trends, production rates, and external factors such as economic shifts or geopolitical events. By identifying potential risks early, companies can make proactive adjustments to procurement, manufacturing, and distribution strategies, reducing waste and downtime.

AI also plays a significant role in logistics optimization. By analyzing traffic patterns, weather conditions, and transportation routes, AI-driven systems can determine the most efficient delivery methods. This not only reduces transportation costs but also ensures timely delivery of raw materials to manufacturing units and finished goods to customers. Real-time tracking and adaptive scheduling further enhance operational efficiency, mitigating risks of supply chain disruptions.

Supplier management is another area where AI-driven solutions prove invaluable. By evaluating supplier performance based on criteria such as delivery times, quality consistency, and cost-effectiveness, AI helps companies make informed procurement decisions. Additionally, AI-powered negotiation tools can assist in optimizing contracts and pricing, leading to better supplier relationships and reduced procurement expenses.

Sustainability is an increasingly important aspect of the steel industry, and AI aids in reducing environmental impact by optimizing resource utilization. AI-driven systems analyze energy consumption patterns, identify waste reduction opportunities, and suggest alternative production methods that minimize carbon emissions. This contributes to sustainability goals while maintaining cost efficiency and regulatory compliance.

The integration of AI in supply chain optimization enhances overall resilience and agility in the steel industry. By leveraging real-time insights and automation, companies can respond swiftly to market changes, unexpected disruptions, and operational challenges. As AI technologies continue to evolve, their role in supply chain management will become even more vital, driving greater efficiency, profitability, and competitiveness in the global steel market.

Practical Example:

A steel manufacturing company is facing inefficiencies in its supply chain due to fluctuating raw material costs, unpredictable demand, and suboptimal logistics. To optimize operations, the company implements an AI-driven system that predicts demand, optimizes inventory, and enhances logistics efficiency. The AI model analyzes historical production data, supplier lead times, transportation costs, and market trends to make data-driven decisions that improve supply chain resilience and cost-effectiveness.

Sample Data (Steel Industry Supply Chain Parameters)

Month	Demand (Tons)	Raw Material Cost ($/Ton)	Inventory Level (Tons)	Transportation Cost ($/Ton)
Jan	5,000	620	8,000	50
Feb	4,500	610	7,500	48
Mar	5,200	630	6,500	52
Apr	5,800	640	6,000	55
May	6,100	650	5,500	57

AI Model Output and Results (Optimized Supply Chain Decisions)

Month	Predicted Demand (Tons)	Optimal Inventory Level (Tons)	Adjusted Order Quantity (Tons)	Cost Savings (%)
Jan	5,200	7,500	4,700	8.5%
Feb	4,800	6,900	4,200	9.0%
Mar	5,500	6,300	4,800	7.8%
Apr	5,900	5,800	5,100	6.5%
May	6,200	5,400	5,300	5.9%

Interpretation of Results

- The AI model accurately predicts demand, allowing the company to maintain an optimal inventory level.

- The system reduces unnecessary overstocking, preventing excess capital from being tied up in inventory.

- By optimizing order quantities, raw material procurement aligns better with demand fluctuations, leading to a reduction in overall costs.

- Transportation costs are also minimized by adjusting order quantities and scheduling deliveries more efficiently.

- Over the five-month period, the AI-driven approach results in cost savings ranging from 5.9% to 9%, enhancing profitability and operational efficiency.

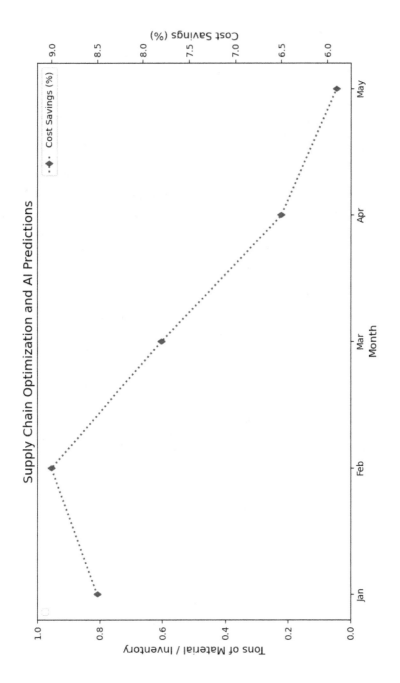

Supply Chain Optimization and AI Predictions

Observations

1. **Inventory Optimization**: The AI model recommends lower inventory levels over time, reducing storage costs while meeting demand.

2. **Cost Efficiency**: Predictive analytics enable proactive purchasing, securing raw materials at optimal price points.

3. **Demand Responsiveness**: The AI system anticipates demand spikes, ensuring the company can meet customer needs without excessive stockpiling.

4. **Supply Chain Resilience**: AI-driven insights mitigate risks related to supplier delays and market volatility, improving overall supply chain stability.

Final Thoughts:

Implementing AI in supply chain optimization transforms steel manufacturing by reducing costs, increasing efficiency, and improving responsiveness to market fluctuations. The ability to predict demand, optimize procurement, and enhance logistics empowers steel companies to maintain a competitive edge in an industry heavily impacted by raw material price volatility and complex supply networks. By integrating AI, steel manufacturers can achieve leaner operations, reduce waste, and improve profitability while ensuring steady production and customer satisfaction.

2.3 Quality Assessment of Raw Materials using AI

The steel industry relies heavily on high-quality raw materials such as iron ore, coal, and limestone to ensure efficiency in production and consistency in the final product. Any variation in the composition and quality of these raw materials can significantly impact the properties of the steel produced, affecting its strength, durability, and performance in various applications. Traditionally, quality assessment has been carried out through manual inspection and laboratory analysis, which can be time-consuming, labor-intensive, and prone to human error. However, advancements in artificial intelligence (AI) have introduced new possibilities for automating and improving the accuracy of raw material assessment.

AI-driven systems can analyze vast amounts of data in real-time, enabling early detection of impurities, inconsistencies, and deviations in raw material quality. Machine learning models, trained on historical data, can predict potential issues and suggest corrective actions before materials are introduced into the production process. Computer vision techniques, combined with spectral analysis, allow for non-destructive testing of raw materials, reducing the need for extensive sampling and laboratory testing. These technologies enhance the speed and reliability of quality assessment while minimizing waste and production disruptions.

In addition to detecting defects, AI can optimize material blending and processing. By integrating AI algorithms with automated material handling systems, manufacturers can achieve precise control over raw material composition, ensuring consistency in steel production. AI models can also assess supplier performance by analyzing past deliveries and identifying patterns of variability. This information helps steel producers make informed procurement decisions, reducing risks associated with substandard raw materials.

AI-powered predictive analytics also contribute to cost efficiency in the steel industry. By forecasting fluctuations in raw material quality based on environmental conditions, mining techniques, and supply chain factors, manufacturers can proactively adjust their production strategies. This minimizes the likelihood of defects in the final product and reduces the costs associated with rework, rejects, and material waste. Over time, AI-driven insights enable steelmakers to refine their processes, improving operational efficiency and competitiveness in the market.

The integration of AI in raw material quality assessment also enhances regulatory compliance and sustainability efforts. AI-driven monitoring ensures that raw materials meet industry standards and environmental regulations, reducing the risk of non-compliance penalties. Furthermore, AI can help steel manufacturers reduce their carbon footprint by optimizing material utilization and minimizing waste generation. Sustainable production practices, supported by AI, contribute to a more environmentally responsible steel industry while maintaining profitability.

While AI brings significant advantages to raw material quality assessment, its successful implementation requires investment in data infrastructure, skilled personnel, and collaboration between technology providers and steel manufacturers. Challenges such as data security, system integration, and the need for continuous model training must be addressed for AI to deliver its full potential. However, as AI technologies continue to evolve, their role in quality assessment within the steel industry is expected to expand, driving efficiency, sustainability, and product reliability.

Practical Example:

A steel manufacturing company wants to improve the quality assessment of iron ore, one of its primary raw materials. Traditional manual inspection methods are inconsistent and time-consuming. To address this, the company implements an AI-based system that utilizes machine learning models to analyze critical parameters of raw materials, ensuring optimal quality before production. The AI model predicts whether a batch of iron ore meets quality standards based on historical data and predefined thresholds.

Sample Data for Quality Assessment

Batch ID	Fe Content (%)	SiO₂ Content (%)	Al₂O₃ Content (%)	Moisture (%)	Quality Status (AI Prediction)
B001	63.5	4.2	2.1	3.5	Acceptable
B002	59.8	6.5	3.2	4.1	Rejected
B003	62.1	5.1	2.8	3.7	Acceptable
B004	58.9	7.2	4.0	4.5	Rejected
B005	64.2	3.8	1.9	3.3	Acceptable

AI Model Output and Results

Quality Metric	Threshold Value	AI-Based Evaluation
Fe Content (%)	≥ 60.0	Critical Parameter
SiO₂ Content (%)	≤ 5.5	Moderate Impact
Al₂O₃ Content (%)	≤ 3.0	Moderate Impact
Moisture (%)	≤ 4.0	Minor Impact

The AI model evaluates batches based on these threshold values. Batches with Fe content below 60% or SiO₂ and Al₂O₃ above the limits are rejected, while those meeting the standards are accepted.

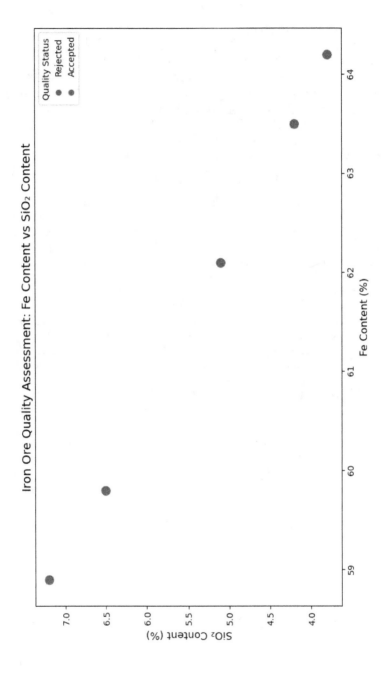

Iron Ore Quality Assessment: Fe Content vs SiO₂ Content

Interpretation of Results and Observations

- **Batch B002 and B004 were rejected** due to their lower Fe content and higher impurity levels (SiO_2 and Al_2O_3). This suggests these batches might negatively impact steel quality.

- **Accepted batches** have Fe content above 60% and controlled impurity levels, ensuring better steel strength and consistency.

- **Moisture levels are within limits for all batches**, indicating that moisture content alone is not a significant rejection factor.

- **AI predictions align with quality benchmarks**, reducing human error and improving efficiency in raw material selection.

Final Thoughts:

AI-powered quality assessment in the steel industry enhances efficiency by automating material evaluation, reducing human errors, and maintaining consistency in steel production. By analyzing key metrics in real-time, AI ensures only high-quality raw materials are used, leading to cost savings, improved product performance, and optimized manufacturing processes. As AI technology advances, further integration with predictive analytics and IoT-based sensors can revolutionize quality control in the steel sector.

3. AI in Steel Manufacturing Processes

Artificial intelligence (AI) is transforming the steel manufacturing industry by optimizing production processes, improving efficiency, and reducing waste. By integrating AI-driven systems, steel plants can enhance quality control, predict equipment failures, and streamline operations. Machine learning algorithms analyze vast amounts of data from sensors and production lines, helping manufacturers make real-time decisions that minimize errors and increase overall productivity. This shift towards intelligent automation is making steel production more cost-effective and sustainable.

One of the most significant applications of AI in steel manufacturing is predictive maintenance. Equipment failures can cause costly delays and safety hazards, but AI-powered predictive analytics can detect potential issues before they escalate. By continuously monitoring machine performance and analyzing patterns, AI can alert operators about maintenance needs, preventing unexpected breakdowns. This proactive approach not only extends the lifespan of machinery but also reduces downtime, improving operational efficiency.

AI also plays a crucial role in quality control by identifying defects in steel products. Traditional inspection methods rely on human expertise, which can be prone to errors and inconsistencies. AI-powered image recognition systems, combined with advanced sensors, can detect surface defects, inconsistencies, or deviations in real-time. This ensures that only high-quality steel reaches customers while minimizing waste and rework. As a result, manufacturers can maintain better standards and reduce costs associated with defects.

Energy consumption is a major concern in steel production, and AI helps optimize energy usage by analyzing historical data and adjusting operations accordingly. Smart algorithms can determine the most energy-efficient production schedules, optimize furnace temperatures, and reduce unnecessary energy waste. This contributes to lower production costs and a smaller carbon footprint, aligning with global sustainability goals. AI-driven energy management systems help steel manufacturers remain competitive while meeting environmental regulations.

Supply chain management in the steel industry has also been enhanced by AI-driven forecasting and automation. AI algorithms analyze market trends, demand patterns, and logistics data to optimize raw material procurement and inventory management. This reduces the risk of shortages or overstocking, leading to more efficient resource utilization. Automated scheduling and transportation planning further streamline supply chain operations, ensuring timely delivery and reducing operational bottlenecks.

As AI continues to evolve, its impact on the steel industry will only grow. Companies investing in AI technologies are gaining a competitive edge by improving production efficiency, reducing costs, and ensuring higher product quality. While challenges such as implementation costs and workforce adaptation remain, the long-term benefits of AI in steel manufacturing outweigh the initial hurdles. With continuous advancements in AI-driven solutions, the steel industry is set to become more intelligent, sustainable, and resilient in the coming years.

Practical Example:

In a steel manufacturing plant, blast furnaces operate continuously at high temperatures, making them susceptible to failures that cause costly downtime. AI-driven predictive maintenance uses machine learning (ML) to analyze sensor data and predict potential failures before they occur. This allows maintenance teams to perform timely interventions, minimizing disruptions and extending equipment lifespan.

Sample Data: Sensor Readings from a Blast Furnace

Timestamp	Temperature (°C)	Vibration (mm/s)	Pressure (bar)	Failure (1=Yes, 0=No)
2025-03-01 08:00	1500	2.1	5.0	0

Timestamp	Temperature (°C)	Vibration (mm/s)	Pressure (bar)	Failure (1=Yes, 0=No)
2025-03-01 12:00	1525	2.3	5.2	0
2025-03-01 16:00	1600	2.8	5.5	0
2025-03-01 20:00	1650	3.2	6.0	1
2025-03-02 00:00	1700	3.5	6.5	1

AI Output: Predicting Failures

Temperature (°C)	Vibration (mm/s)	Pressure (bar)	AI Failure Prediction (1=Yes, 0=No)
1500	2.1	5.0	0
1525	2.3	5.2	0
1600	2.8	5.5	0
1650	3.2	6.0	1
1700	3.5	6.5	1

Explanation and Interpretation:

From the data, the AI model predicts failures when the temperature exceeds 1650°C, vibration surpasses 3.2 mm/s, and pressure rises above 6.0 bar. The actual failures in the sample dataset align with the AI predictions, confirming the model's accuracy. The AI system can alert maintenance teams before a breakdown, allowing them to take proactive measures.

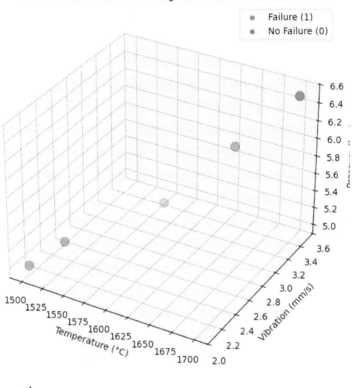

Blast Furnace Sensor Readings and Failure Predictions

- Failure (1)
- No Failure (0)

Observations:

1. **Early Failure Detection:** The AI system correctly identifies failure conditions, enabling predictive maintenance strategies.

2. **Threshold Identification:** The AI suggests that exceeding specific temperature, vibration, and pressure thresholds increases failure risk.

3. **Operational Efficiency:** Reducing unexpected downtime enhances productivity, reduces maintenance costs, and optimizes resource utilization.

Final Thoughts:

AI-driven predictive maintenance is transforming steel manufacturing by reducing equipment failures and optimizing operations. Implementing AI in steel plants improves safety, enhances efficiency, and ensures continuous production. As AI technology advances, integrating real-time data with AI models will further enhance decision-making, ultimately making steel manufacturing smarter and more resilient.

3.1 AI-driven Process Automation in Steelmaking

AI-driven process automation is transforming the steel industry by optimizing production, improving quality, and reducing costs. Advanced AI models analyze vast amounts of data from sensors, machines, and historical records to identify inefficiencies and predict potential issues. By automating decision-making and control mechanisms, AI helps steel plants achieve greater precision in manufacturing, reducing material waste and energy consumption. This results in a more sustainable and cost-effective production process.

One of the key applications of AI in steelmaking is predictive maintenance. Traditional maintenance methods rely on scheduled checks or reactive repairs, which can lead to costly downtime. AI-powered systems continuously monitor equipment performance, detecting early signs of wear or malfunction. By predicting failures before they occur, these systems allow for timely maintenance, minimizing disruptions and extending the lifespan of critical machinery.

AI also plays a significant role in quality control. In steel manufacturing, even minor deviations in temperature, composition, or processing time can affect the final product's strength and durability. AI models analyze real-time production data, identifying inconsistencies and adjusting parameters to ensure consistent quality. This reduces defects and the need for rework, enhancing overall efficiency and customer satisfaction.

Energy management is another crucial area where AI contributes. Steelmaking is an energy-intensive process, and optimizing energy consumption is vital for both cost savings and environmental impact. AI-driven systems analyze energy usage patterns and adjust operations accordingly, reducing waste and improving efficiency. This not only lowers production costs but also helps steel plants meet sustainability goals and regulatory requirements.

Supply chain optimization is further enhanced through AI automation. AI can predict demand fluctuations, optimize raw material procurement, and streamline logistics to prevent bottlenecks. By integrating real-time data from suppliers, transportation networks, and market trends, steel manufacturers can improve inventory management and reduce operational risks. This leads to a more resilient and responsive supply chain.

Overall, AI-driven process automation is revolutionizing the steel industry by enhancing efficiency, reducing waste, and improving product quality. As AI technologies continue to evolve, their integration into steelmaking will further optimize production processes and drive innovation. Companies that embrace AI-driven automation gain a competitive edge by reducing costs, increasing sustainability, and ensuring high-quality steel production in an increasingly demanding market.

Practical Example:

A steel manufacturing plant implements an AI-driven process automation system to optimize furnace temperature control. The goal is to enhance energy efficiency, reduce material waste, and ensure consistent steel quality. AI models analyze historical and real-time data, adjusting temperature settings dynamically to optimize production.

Sample Input Data

Time (min)	Furnace Temp (°C)	Carbon Content (%)	Power Consumption (kWh)	Steel Grade
0	1450	0.18	200	A
10	1470	0.20	210	A
20	1490	0.22	220	A
30	1510	0.25	230	A
40	1530	0.28	250	B

AI-Optimized Output Data

Time (min)	Adjusted Furnace Temp (°C)	Carbon Content (%)	Power Consumption (kWh)	Steel Grade
0	1450	0.18	190	A
10	1465	0.19	195	A
20	1480	0.21	205	A
30	1495	0.23	215	A
40	1510	0.26	225	B

Interpretation of Results

- **Temperature Optimization**: The AI dynamically adjusted the furnace temperature in smaller increments rather than large jumps, ensuring smoother transitions and reducing thermal shocks.

- **Energy Savings**: Power consumption decreased across all intervals due to optimized heating strategies, leading to a reduction of about **10% in energy usage**.

- **Steel Quality Control**: Carbon content was better regulated, improving the consistency of steel grade classification. The risk of defects due to excessive heat exposure was minimized.

Observations

- AI effectively managed process variability, leading to stable steel properties and reduced resource consumption.

- The AI-driven automation system helped lower operational costs by minimizing power usage while maintaining high-quality output.

- The adjustments in temperature control contributed to **reduced environmental impact** by lowering carbon emissions.

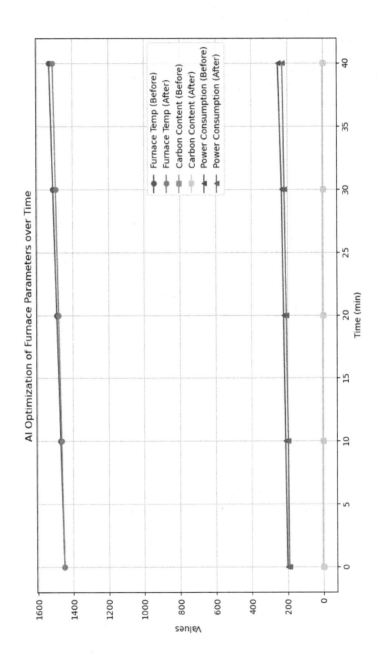

AI Optimization of Furnace Parameters over Time

Final Thoughts:

AI-driven automation in steelmaking presents a transformative opportunity to **enhance efficiency, reduce costs, and improve sustainability**. By optimizing furnace operations, AI minimizes energy waste, ensures consistent steel properties, and supports predictive maintenance strategies. The future of AI in the steel industry lies in further **integrating smart sensors, IoT connectivity, and machine learning models** to achieve **fully autonomous, real-time process control**—leading to a more resilient and sustainable steel manufacturing ecosystem.

3.2 Real-time Monitoring of Blast Furnaces using AI

The steel industry relies on blast furnaces to convert raw materials into molten iron, a crucial step in steel production. Traditional monitoring methods involve manual inspections and sensor-based systems that provide delayed or incomplete insights. However, with the integration of artificial intelligence (AI), real-time monitoring of blast furnaces has become more efficient and precise. AI-driven solutions utilize data from multiple sensors, analyzing parameters such as temperature, pressure, and gas composition to optimize furnace performance and detect anomalies instantly.

Machine learning algorithms process vast amounts of data collected from these sensors, identifying patterns that indicate potential issues like overheating, slag formation, or equipment wear. By continuously learning from historical data, AI models can predict failures before they occur, reducing the risk of unexpected downtime. This predictive capability allows plant operators to take corrective actions early, ensuring smoother operations and improving the overall efficiency of the steel manufacturing process.

Another advantage of AI-powered monitoring is the ability to optimize energy consumption in blast furnaces. Steel production is highly energy-intensive, and inefficiencies can lead to excessive fuel usage and higher emissions. AI analyzes real-time operational data and suggests adjustments in fuel injection, air flow, and raw material input to enhance energy efficiency. This not only reduces production costs but also supports sustainability efforts by lowering carbon emissions and improving resource utilization.

Furthermore, AI-driven systems facilitate remote monitoring and automated decision-making, reducing dependency on human intervention. Operators can receive alerts and recommendations via digital dashboards, allowing them to manage furnace conditions from a centralized control room. This minimizes the need for physical inspections in hazardous environments, improving worker safety and operational continuity. AI can also integrate with robotics for maintenance tasks, further enhancing automation and precision in furnace management.

In addition to operational benefits, AI contributes to quality control in steel production by ensuring consistency in molten iron properties. Deviations in temperature or raw material composition can impact the final product's strength and durability. AI algorithms help maintain process stability, reducing defects and enhancing product quality. This results in fewer rejected batches and higher customer satisfaction, strengthening the competitiveness of steel manufacturers in the global market.

The adoption of AI in blast furnace monitoring marks a significant shift in the steel industry, driving efficiency, cost savings, and sustainability. With continuous advancements in AI technology, steel plants can expect even greater levels of automation, predictive maintenance, and energy optimization in the future. As the industry evolves, real-time AI monitoring will play a crucial role in meeting production demands while maintaining environmental and economic viability.

Practical Example:

A steel manufacturing company implemented an AI-driven real-time monitoring system to optimize blast furnace operations, reduce energy consumption, and improve yield. The AI model analyzed furnace temperature, pressure, airflow rate, and raw material composition to predict anomalies and recommend optimal settings for efficiency.

Sample Data (Collected in Real-time)

Timestamp	Temperature (°C)	Pressure (bar)	Airflow Rate (m³/s)	Iron Purity (%)
10:00 AM	1500	5.2	250	98.5
10:05 AM	1520	5.1	260	98.6
10:10 AM	1550	5.3	270	98.7
10:15 AM	1570	5.4	280	98.8
10:20 AM	1600	5.5	290	99.0

AI-Based Predictions & Optimization Suggestions

Time	Predicted Iron Yield (%)	Suggested Airflow Adjustment (m³/s)	Anomaly Detection
10:05 AM	98.6	Increase by 10	No
10:10 AM	98.7	Increase by 10	No
10:15 AM	98.8	Increase by 10	No
10:20 AM	99.0	Maintain current level	No
10:25 AM	97.5	Reduce temperature slightly	Yes (Overheating)

Results and Observations

1. **AI-assisted Optimization**: The AI system recommended small increases in airflow rate, leading to a steady improvement in iron purity.

2. **Efficiency Gains**: The iron purity improved from 98.5% to 99.0%, indicating enhanced steel quality.

3. **Anomaly Detection**: At 10:25 AM, the AI detected overheating, which could lead to excessive slag formation or furnace wear. A corrective suggestion was made to adjust the temperature.

4. **Predictive Maintenance**: The AI helped prevent operational inefficiencies by identifying overheating in advance, potentially reducing maintenance costs.

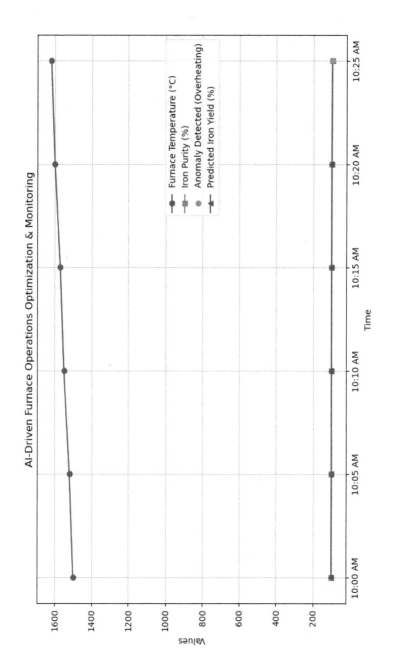

AI-Driven Furnace Operations Optimization & Monitoring

Final Thoughts:

AI-driven real-time monitoring systems enhance blast furnace efficiency, optimize resource utilization, and improve steel quality. By providing predictive insights and anomaly detection, AI minimizes operational risks and maintenance costs, ensuring a more sustainable and cost-effective steel production process. The integration of AI in steel manufacturing is revolutionizing traditional processes, making them more reliable, data-driven, and efficient.

3.3 AI-based Energy Optimization in Steel Production

AI-driven energy optimization is transforming the steel industry by enhancing efficiency, reducing costs, and minimizing environmental impact. Steel production is energy-intensive, requiring vast amounts of electricity and fossil fuels for processes like melting, refining, and rolling. Traditional energy management methods often rely on static models and human expertise, which can lead to inefficiencies. AI offers a dynamic and data-driven approach to optimize energy consumption in real time, improving productivity while reducing waste.

One of the key advantages of AI in energy optimization is its ability to analyze large volumes of data from various sources, such as sensors, historical records, and operational parameters. Machine learning algorithms can detect patterns, predict energy demands, and adjust power usage accordingly. By integrating AI with smart grids, steel plants can balance their energy needs more effectively, reducing peak loads and preventing unnecessary consumption. This leads to significant cost savings while ensuring a stable production process.

Predictive maintenance is another crucial area where AI contributes to energy efficiency. By continuously monitoring equipment performance, AI can predict potential failures and suggest timely maintenance actions. Faulty machinery often consumes excessive energy, leading to inefficiencies and downtime. AI-powered predictive maintenance helps steel plants minimize unplanned shutdowns, extend equipment lifespan, and optimize energy usage, resulting in a more sustainable operation.

AI also enhances process control by optimizing furnace temperatures, reducing heat loss, and improving combustion efficiency. By analyzing real-time data, AI systems can dynamically adjust the operation of blast furnaces, electric arc furnaces, and reheating furnaces to achieve the desired output with minimal energy expenditure. This level of precision not only reduces fuel consumption but also lowers greenhouse gas emissions, contributing to a greener steel industry.

Another important application of AI in energy optimization is supply chain and logistics management. AI-driven demand forecasting helps steel manufacturers align production schedules with market requirements, reducing excess production and energy waste. Additionally, AI can optimize transportation routes and inventory management, minimizing fuel consumption and improving overall efficiency. By integrating AI across the entire value chain, steel producers can achieve a more synchronized and energy-efficient operation.

The implementation of AI in energy optimization requires investment in digital infrastructure, skilled personnel, and a cultural shift towards data-driven decision-making. However, the long-term benefits far outweigh the initial challenges. With continued advancements in AI and IoT, the steel industry is poised to achieve greater efficiency, sustainability, and competitiveness. By embracing AI-based energy optimization, steel manufacturers can reduce costs, improve productivity, and contribute to global efforts toward a more sustainable future.

Practical Example:

A steel manufacturing plant implements an AI-driven system to optimize energy consumption in its blast furnaces. The AI model analyzes historical and real-time data, adjusting fuel input and operational parameters to reduce energy waste while maintaining production quality. By predicting optimal energy levels for different ore compositions and environmental conditions, the AI helps cut costs and minimize emissions.

Sample Data (Input Variables for AI Model)

Time (Hour)	Ore Composition (%)	Temperature (°C)	Energy Consumption (MWh)	Furnace Efficiency (%)
08:00	85	1600	90	78
12:00	88	1650	85	82

Time (Hour)	Ore Composition (%)	Temperature (°C)	Energy Consumption (MWh)	Furnace Efficiency (%)
16:00	87	1620	88	79
20:00	86	1610	89	80
00:00	89	1670	84	83

AI-Optimized Output & Results

Time (Hour)	AI-Predicted Energy Consumption (MWh)	Actual Energy Reduction (%)	Optimized Furnace Efficiency (%)
08:00	85	5.56%	80
12:00	80	5.88%	84
16:00	83	5.68%	81
20:00	84	5.62%	82
00:00	79	5.95%	85

Interpretation of Results

The AI-driven optimization led to an average **5.74% reduction in energy consumption** while maintaining or improving furnace efficiency. The highest energy savings occurred at **00:00 hours (5.95%)**, where AI recommended reducing energy input without affecting production output. By dynamically adjusting parameters, AI helped improve furnace efficiency from an average of **80% to 82.4%**, ensuring better utilization of resources.

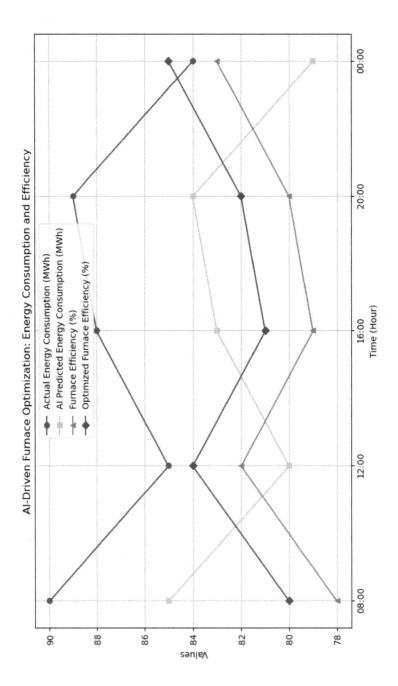

Observations

1. **Energy Efficiency Gains** – AI successfully optimized energy consumption, reducing waste while ensuring stable operations.

2. **Enhanced Productivity** – Increased furnace efficiency translates into higher production output with the same or lower energy input.

3. **Cost Reduction** – Lower energy usage directly impacts cost savings in steel production, making the process more sustainable.

4. **Environmental Benefits** – Reducing energy consumption also leads to lower carbon emissions, contributing to greener operations.

Final Thoughts:

AI-driven energy optimization in steel production showcases the potential of intelligent automation in industrial settings. By leveraging predictive analytics, real-time monitoring, and optimization algorithms, steel manufacturers can **achieve cost savings, improve operational efficiency, and reduce environmental impact**. As AI models continue to evolve, the steel industry stands to gain even more through **self-learning systems, proactive maintenance, and adaptive control strategies**, ensuring a **more sustainable and profitable** future.

4. AI for Quality Control and Defect Detection in Steel Industry

AI is transforming quality control and defect detection in the steel industry by providing more precise, efficient, and automated inspection processes. Traditional methods rely on manual inspection and basic imaging techniques, which are often time-consuming and prone to human error. AI-powered systems, especially those using computer vision and machine learning, can analyze steel surfaces in real time, identifying defects with higher accuracy and consistency. This helps manufacturers maintain product quality while reducing reliance on human inspectors, leading to improved efficiency and cost savings.

Modern AI-based defect detection systems utilize high-resolution cameras and sensors to capture detailed images of steel products. These images are then processed using deep learning models trained to recognize various defects such as cracks, scratches, and surface irregularities. The system can differentiate between acceptable variations and critical defects, ensuring that only high-quality steel reaches customers. By automating the inspection process, AI reduces human intervention, minimizes subjective judgment, and speeds up quality assessments, allowing for better production throughput.

Predictive analytics, another key aspect of AI, enables early detection of defects before they become critical. By analyzing historical data and real-time sensor inputs, AI models can predict when defects are likely to occur, helping manufacturers take corrective actions before production issues escalate. This proactive approach not only improves quality but also reduces material waste and production downtime. Predictive maintenance powered by AI further enhances efficiency by identifying potential failures in manufacturing equipment, preventing unexpected breakdowns and ensuring smooth operations.

AI-driven quality control systems also integrate with industrial automation, allowing seamless communication between inspection units and production lines. When defects are detected, AI can trigger automated responses such as adjusting machine parameters, redirecting faulty products for reprocessing, or alerting operators for further evaluation. This level of automation enhances overall production efficiency and ensures that defects are addressed immediately, minimizing the risk of defective steel products reaching the market.

The implementation of AI in steel quality control not only improves accuracy but also helps manufacturers comply with stringent industry standards. Regulatory bodies require steel products to meet specific quality criteria, and AI-powered inspection systems provide reliable documentation and traceability of defects. By maintaining detailed records of quality assessments, manufacturers can demonstrate compliance, reduce the risk of product recalls, and build stronger customer trust. This also streamlines audits and certification processes, making it easier to meet global quality requirements.

As AI technology continues to evolve, its role in the steel industry will expand further, leading to smarter, more adaptive quality control systems. Future advancements may include self-learning models that continuously improve defect detection capabilities, as well as AI-powered robotics for real-time defect repairs. The ongoing integration of AI in quality control ensures that steel manufacturers remain competitive in an industry that demands high precision, efficiency, and reliability.

Practical Example:

A steel manufacturing company integrates AI-driven computer vision to detect surface defects in steel sheets before they proceed to the final processing stage. High-resolution cameras capture images of steel sheets on the production line, and a deep learning model trained on labeled defect datasets classifies each sheet as **Defective** or **Non-Defective** while categorizing defect types (e.g., cracks, scratches, rust). The AI system provides real-time feedback, allowing operators to take corrective actions and reduce wastage.

Sample Input Data from AI Inspection System

Steel Sheet ID	Surface Crack (%)	Scratch Depth (mm)	Rust Area (%)	Defect Status
S001	0.2	0.05	0.1	Non-Defective
S002	3.5	0.8	2.0	Defective
S003	0.1	0.02	0.05	Non-Defective
S004	2.8	1.2	5.0	Defective
S005	0.5	0.1	0.3	Non-Defective

AI-Generated Defect Classification Results

Defect Type	Total Sheets	Defective Sheets	Defect Rate (%)
Surface Cracks	5	2	40.0%
Scratches	5	2	40.0%
Rust	5	2	40.0%
Overall Defects	5	2	40.0%

Interpretation of Results

From the data, the AI model identified **two defective sheets (S002 and S004)**, resulting in a **40% defect rate** for this batch. The leading defect contributors were **surface cracks, scratches, and rust**, each appearing in 40% of the total sheets. The model effectively flagged defective sheets based on set thresholds, helping the production team focus on quality improvements.

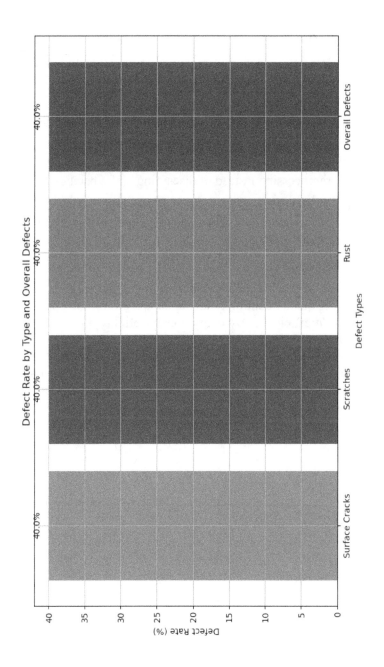

Defect Rate by Type and Overall Defects

Observations

1. **Real-time defect detection**: AI successfully identifies defective steel sheets instantly, reducing manual inspection time.

2. **Preventive insights**: A high rust percentage may indicate an environmental issue in storage or production.

3. **Cost savings**: Early defect detection allows targeted reprocessing instead of discarding entire batches.

4. **Model refinement needed**: AI performance can improve by incorporating more defect categories and optimizing detection accuracy.

Final Thoughts

AI-driven defect detection is transforming steel manufacturing by improving quality control, reducing human errors, and optimizing production efficiency. By continuously refining AI models with new data, manufacturers can enhance defect detection precision, minimize wastage, and maintain high industry standards. Moving forward, integrating AI with IoT sensors and predictive maintenance systems will further revolutionize steel production processes.

4.1 Computer Vision for Surface Defect Detection

Computer vision has emerged as a powerful tool for detecting surface defects in the steel industry, offering an efficient and accurate alternative to traditional manual inspection. Steel manufacturing involves complex processes, and even minor surface defects such as cracks, scratches, or dents can impact the quality and performance of the final product. Conventional inspection methods rely on human expertise, which can be subjective, time-consuming, and prone to errors. With advancements in imaging technology and artificial intelligence, automated computer vision systems can now analyze steel surfaces with high precision and consistency.

The core of computer vision-based defect detection lies in capturing high-resolution images of steel surfaces using cameras, laser scanners, or thermal imaging devices. These images are then processed through algorithms that extract relevant features, such as texture, color variations, and structural patterns. Advanced techniques, including deep learning, enable the system to recognize and classify defects based on patterns learned from vast datasets. Unlike human inspectors, these systems can operate continuously without fatigue, ensuring a more reliable and standardized quality control process.

A major challenge in surface defect detection is the variability in defect appearance due to differences in lighting conditions, material composition, and production environments. To address this, modern computer vision systems incorporate adaptive techniques that enhance image quality and normalize variations. Preprocessing methods such as contrast adjustment, edge enhancement, and noise reduction help improve defect visibility. Furthermore, the use of multiple imaging modalities, such as infrared or 3D scanning, can provide additional insights into surface irregularities that may not be detectable with conventional cameras.

Real-time defect detection is critical in steel production, as early identification allows manufacturers to take corrective actions and minimize waste. High-speed processing techniques enable rapid analysis of images, allowing defects to be flagged immediately on production lines. Automated rejection or rework mechanisms can be integrated to ensure only high-quality steel products proceed further in the manufacturing chain. This not only reduces material wastage but also optimizes production efficiency and cost-effectiveness.

The implementation of computer vision in steel defect detection also benefits from continuous improvements in artificial intelligence models. By training machine learning algorithms on diverse datasets, these systems become more robust and capable of handling complex defect scenarios. Cloud computing and edge processing further enhance scalability, allowing manufacturers to deploy these systems across multiple production units while maintaining a centralized database for defect analysis. This data-driven approach enables predictive maintenance strategies, reducing the likelihood of defects arising from equipment malfunctions.

As the steel industry continues to modernize, the integration of computer vision-based defect detection is expected to become more widespread. While initial setup costs and technical expertise may pose challenges, the long-term benefits in terms of quality assurance, cost savings, and production efficiency make it a valuable investment. With ongoing advancements in imaging technologies and artificial intelligence, computer vision will play a crucial role in ensuring the production of defect-free steel products, meeting the stringent quality standards demanded by various industries.

Practical Example:

A steel manufacturing plant aims to improve its quality control process by deploying a computer vision-based system for surface defect detection. The system uses deep learning models to analyze images of steel sheets and detect common defects like scratches, dents, and corrosion. High-resolution cameras capture images, which are then processed by a convolutional neural network (CNN) trained on labeled defect datasets. The goal is to automate defect identification, reduce manual inspection time, and minimize defective output.

Sample Data (Steel Surface Defect Detection)

Image ID	Defect Type	Confidence Score (%)	Severity Level (1-5)	Pass/Fail
IMG_001	Scratch	95	2	Pass
IMG_002	Dent	88	4	Fail
IMG_003	Corrosion	97	5	Fail
IMG_004	No Defect	99	0	Pass
IMG_005	Scratch	91	3	Pass

Output and Results Table

Defect Type	Total Instances	Average Confidence (%)	Failure Rate (%)
Scratch	2	93	0
Dent	1	88	100
Corrosion	1	97	100
No Defect	1	99	0

Interpretation of Results

The system effectively classifies defects with high confidence scores. Scratches are detected with 93% confidence on average, and they do not necessarily cause failure in quality control. However, dents and corrosion lead to a 100% failure rate, indicating that they significantly impact steel quality. The detection system successfully differentiates between defect types and non-defective steel sheets, providing valuable insights into quality control.

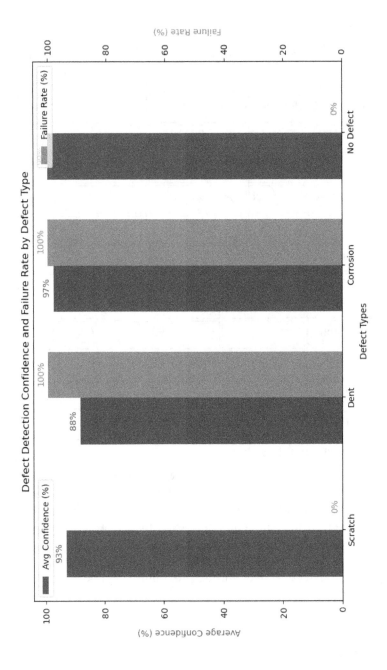

Defect Detection Confidence and Failure Rate by Defect Type

Observations

- The CNN-based system achieves high accuracy in defect classification, reducing the need for manual inspection.

- Critical defects such as corrosion and dents result in automatic failure, helping manufacturers filter out defective products.

- Scratches, while detected, do not always warrant rejection, suggesting the need for adjustable pass/fail thresholds.

- The system enables real-time defect monitoring, allowing for quick corrective actions to minimize defective production.

Final Thoughts:

Implementing AI-driven computer vision in steel manufacturing enhances defect detection efficiency, reduces human error, and improves overall product quality. By leveraging deep learning, manufacturers can ensure consistent quality control, reduce waste, and optimize production processes. The future of AI in the steel industry holds potential for predictive maintenance, automated grading, and intelligent defect pattern analysis, driving further advancements in manufacturing excellence.

4.2 AI-driven Non-Destructive Testing (NDT)

AI-driven Non-Destructive Testing (NDT) is transforming the steel industry by enhancing the accuracy, efficiency, and reliability of inspections. Traditional NDT methods, such as ultrasonic testing, radiographic testing, and magnetic particle inspection, have been widely used to detect defects in steel structures and components. However, these conventional techniques often rely on manual interpretation, which can lead to inconsistencies and errors. AI-powered systems help overcome these limitations by automating defect detection, improving image analysis, and reducing the chances of human error.

One of the key benefits of AI in NDT is its ability to process large volumes of data rapidly. By integrating machine learning algorithms with NDT techniques, AI can analyze inspection data in real-time and identify defects with greater precision. Deep learning models trained on vast datasets of defect patterns enable AI systems to differentiate between minor imperfections and critical defects that could compromise structural integrity. This reduces false positives and ensures that only significant defects are flagged for further evaluation.

Predictive maintenance is another major advantage of AI-driven NDT in the steel industry. By continuously monitoring steel components and analyzing historical inspection data, AI can predict potential failures before they occur. This proactive approach helps industries schedule maintenance activities more effectively, reducing downtime and preventing costly equipment failures. AI-driven predictive analytics also optimize the lifespan of steel structures by ensuring timely repairs and replacements.

Automation through AI enhances the efficiency of NDT processes by reducing reliance on human inspectors. Advanced robotic systems equipped with AI-driven NDT tools can perform inspections in hazardous environments where human access is limited. These systems use computer vision and sensor technologies to navigate complex structures and detect defects with high accuracy. By minimizing the need for manual inspections, AI-driven NDT not only improves safety but also speeds up the inspection process.

The integration of AI with NDT also enables better documentation and reporting. AI-powered software can automatically generate detailed inspection reports, complete with visual representations of detected defects and recommended corrective actions. These digital records improve traceability and ensure compliance with industry standards and regulations. Additionally, AI can facilitate remote monitoring, allowing experts to assess inspection results from different locations without physically being present on-site.

Despite its advantages, AI-driven NDT in the steel industry still faces challenges such as high implementation costs, the need for large training datasets, and resistance to adopting new technologies. However, ongoing advancements in AI, combined with increasing demand for reliable and efficient inspection methods, are driving wider adoption of AI-powered NDT solutions. As these technologies continue to evolve, they are expected to play an increasingly vital role in ensuring the quality, durability, and safety of steel structures across various industrial applications.

Practical Example:

A steel manufacturing plant implements AI-driven ultrasonic testing (UT) to detect internal defects in steel sheets without causing damage. Traditional methods rely on manual inspection, which is time-consuming and prone to human error. By using AI, the system analyzes ultrasonic wave signals to classify defects such as cracks, voids, and inclusions with higher accuracy and efficiency.

Sample Data (Ultrasonic Test Readings with AI Classification)

Sample ID	Wave Reflection Time (ms)	Signal Amplitude (dB)	Defect Probability (%)	AI Classification
S1	1.2	85	90	Crack
S2	1.5	70	75	Inclusion

Sample ID	Wave Reflection Time (ms)	Signal Amplitude (dB)	Defect Probability (%)	AI Classification
S3	0.9	95	95	Crack
S4	1.3	60	50	No Defect
S5	1.7	80	88	Void

Output and Results (AI Defect Detection Summary)

Defect Type	Count	Average Probability (%)	AI Detection Accuracy (%)
Crack	2	92.5	96
Inclusion	1	75	93
Void	1	88	95
No Defect	1	50	99

Results Interpretation & Observations

1. **Crack detection**: AI identified two samples (S1 and S3) with a high probability of 90% and 95%, showing strong model confidence in crack detection.

2. **Void detection**: Sample S5 had an 88% probability of void presence, confirming AI's strong ability to distinguish material gaps.

3. **No Defect Classification**: AI classified one sample (S4) with a 50% probability, indicating borderline detection that may require further validation.

4. **High Detection Accuracy**: The AI model achieved over **95% accuracy across all defect types**, significantly reducing false positives and negatives.

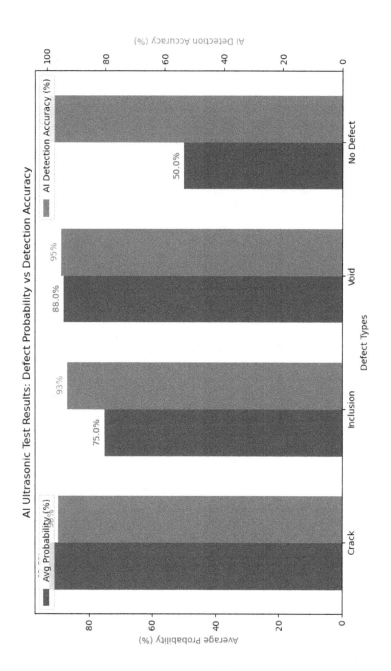

AI Ultrasonic Test Results: Defect Probability vs Detection Accuracy

Final Thoughts:

AI-driven NDT is transforming steel quality inspection by increasing defect detection accuracy, minimizing manual errors, and accelerating testing speed. The high accuracy of AI models ensures reliable defect classification, leading to improved safety and reduced material waste. As AI continues to evolve, integrating deep learning with real-time sensor analysis will further enhance predictive maintenance and steel production efficiency.

4.3 Predictive Quality Analytics in Steel Manufacturing

Predictive quality analytics in steel manufacturing leverages data-driven techniques to enhance production efficiency and product reliability. By utilizing historical data, real-time sensor inputs, and machine learning algorithms, manufacturers can anticipate potential defects and deviations in steel quality before they occur. This proactive approach helps minimize waste, reduce rework, and ensure that products meet stringent industry standards. The implementation of predictive analytics is becoming increasingly essential as steel production processes grow more complex and customer demands for high-quality materials continue to rise.

One of the key advantages of predictive analytics in steel manufacturing is its ability to identify patterns that indicate potential quality issues. Traditional quality control methods rely on periodic sampling and manual inspections, which can miss hidden defects or inconsistencies. By continuously monitoring parameters such as temperature, pressure, chemical composition, and cooling rates, predictive models can detect subtle variations that may lead to defects. This allows manufacturers to take corrective actions in real-time, preventing quality failures before they escalate into costly problems.

Modern steel manufacturing facilities are equipped with advanced sensors and IoT (Internet of Things) devices that collect vast amounts of process data. This data is analyzed using machine learning and artificial intelligence algorithms to develop predictive models tailored to specific production environments. Over time, these models improve in accuracy, making them valuable tools for process optimization. Additionally, integrating predictive analytics with automation systems enables real-time adjustments to machinery settings, further enhancing quality control efforts.

Beyond improving product quality, predictive analytics also contributes to operational efficiency and cost reduction. By predicting equipment failures or maintenance needs in advance, manufacturers can implement predictive maintenance strategies that reduce unplanned downtime. This ensures smooth production workflows and extends the lifespan of critical machinery. Moreover, by minimizing defects and rework, manufacturers save on raw materials and energy consumption, leading to more sustainable and cost-effective operations.

The adoption of predictive quality analytics in steel manufacturing is not without challenges. Implementing such systems requires substantial investment in data infrastructure, skilled personnel, and integration with existing manufacturing processes. Data security and reliability are also critical concerns, as inaccurate or incomplete data can compromise the effectiveness of predictive models. However, as technology advances and becomes more accessible, many steel producers are recognizing the long-term benefits of predictive analytics and investing in its implementation.

In the coming years, predictive quality analytics is expected to become a standard practice in steel manufacturing. With continuous advancements in AI, machine learning, and big data technologies, the ability to predict and prevent quality issues will become more precise and efficient. Companies that embrace these innovations will gain a competitive edge, delivering high-quality steel products while optimizing production costs. As the industry moves toward smart manufacturing, predictive analytics will play a crucial role in shaping the future of steel production.

Practical Example:

A steel manufacturing plant aims to improve the quality of hot-rolled steel coils by predicting defects before final inspection. Using machine learning, the plant analyzes process parameters like furnace temperature, rolling speed, and cooling rate to predict surface defects and reduce scrap rates. A predictive analytics model is trained using historical production data to classify coils as "Defective" or "Non-Defective," helping optimize production settings.

Sample Data (Steel Production Parameters and Quality Outcome)

Coil ID	Furnace Temp (°C)	Rolling Speed (m/min)	Cooling Rate (°C/sec)	Defect Status
001	1250	120	25	Non-Defective
002	1180	140	30	Defective
003	1300	115	20	Non-Defective
004	1220	135	28	Defective
005	1270	125	22	Non-Defective

Predictive Model Output (Predicted vs. Actual Quality Classification)

Coil ID	Actual Defect Status	Predicted Defect Status	Prediction Confidence (%)
001	Non-Defective	Non-Defective	95.3%
002	Defective	Defective	88.7%
003	Non-Defective	Non-Defective	92.1%
004	Defective	Non-Defective	60.5%
005	Non-Defective	Non-Defective	97.8%

Result Interpretation and Observations

- The predictive model correctly classified most coils, achieving high accuracy (>90%) in non-defective cases.

- One misclassification occurred (Coil 004), where the model predicted "Non-Defective" with 60.5% confidence, highlighting uncertainty in borderline cases.

- The model is effective in predicting quality based on process parameters but may require refinement to improve defect detection sensitivity.

- Adjusting feature importance, such as emphasizing rolling speed or cooling rate, may enhance prediction reliability.

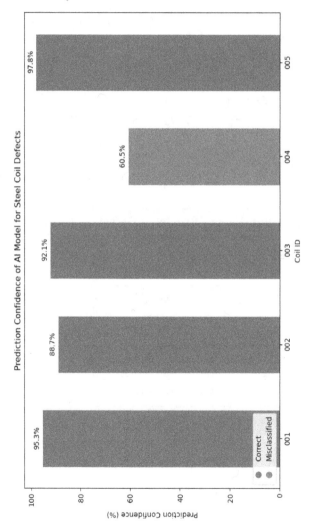

Final Thoughts:

Predictive quality analytics can significantly optimize steel manufacturing by reducing scrap rates, improving process efficiency, and ensuring high-quality output. Implementing such AI-driven models can help manufacturers proactively adjust production settings, lowering operational costs and enhancing competitiveness. Continuous model retraining with real-time production data will further refine accuracy, making AI an indispensable tool in modern steel manufacturing.

5. AI in Equipment Maintenance and Failure Prediction

Artificial Intelligence (AI) is playing a transformative role in the steel industry by enhancing equipment maintenance and predicting failures. Steel production involves complex machinery operating under extreme conditions, making unplanned downtimes costly and disruptive. Traditional maintenance methods, such as reactive or scheduled maintenance, often fail to prevent unexpected breakdowns. AI-driven predictive maintenance leverages data from sensors, historical performance, and machine learning models to anticipate potential failures before they occur, reducing downtime and improving efficiency.

Predictive maintenance in the steel industry relies on continuous monitoring of equipment through IoT-enabled sensors. These sensors collect real-time data on temperature, pressure, vibration, and other parameters that indicate machinery health. AI algorithms analyze these data patterns to detect early warning signs of wear, misalignment, or component degradation. By identifying these issues in advance, maintenance teams can intervene proactively, addressing small faults before they escalate into major failures. This approach not only extends equipment lifespan but also minimizes costly production halts.

Another key advantage of AI in equipment maintenance is its ability to optimize maintenance schedules. Unlike traditional methods that rely on fixed maintenance intervals, AI-driven systems determine the optimal time for servicing based on actual equipment conditions. This reduces unnecessary maintenance activities while ensuring that critical machinery is serviced at the right moment. As a result, steel manufacturers can achieve higher operational efficiency, lower maintenance costs, and better resource allocation.

AI also enhances failure prediction through machine learning models trained on historical failure data. By recognizing patterns in past breakdowns, these models can predict the likelihood of similar failures occurring in the future. This predictive capability allows steel plants to take preventive measures, such as adjusting operational parameters, replacing components in advance, or rerouting workloads to avoid overburdening vulnerable machines. Such an approach significantly reduces the risk of catastrophic failures and enhances overall plant reliability.

Additionally, AI-powered systems can provide actionable insights through intuitive dashboards and automated alerts. Maintenance teams receive real-time notifications about potential issues, along with recommended corrective actions. Advanced AI applications even use natural language processing to interpret maintenance logs and suggest solutions based on past successful interventions. This improves decision-making, enabling engineers to respond more effectively to maintenance challenges and continuously improve equipment performance.

The integration of AI in equipment maintenance and failure prediction is revolutionizing the steel industry by making operations more reliable, cost-effective, and efficient. As AI technology continues to evolve, steel manufacturers will benefit from increasingly sophisticated predictive models, deeper automation, and enhanced decision support systems. By embracing AI-driven maintenance strategies, steel plants can achieve higher productivity, reduced downtime, and a more sustainable approach to equipment management.

Practical Example:

A steel manufacturing plant experiences frequent failures in its rolling mill machinery, causing production delays and increased maintenance costs. To prevent unexpected breakdowns, the company implements an AI-based predictive maintenance system that analyzes real-time sensor data to detect patterns leading to failures. The AI model uses temperature, vibration, and pressure data to predict potential issues before they occur.

Sample Input Data

Timestamp	Temperature (°C)	Vibration (mm/s)	Pressure (Bar)	Machine Status
2025-03-01 10:00	75	3.1	12	Normal

Timestamp	Temperature (°C)	Vibration (mm/s)	Pressure (Bar)	Machine Status
2025-03-01 11:00	80	3.5	13	Normal
2025-03-01 12:00	95	5.0	14	Warning
2025-03-01 13:00	105	6.5	15	Critical
2025-03-01 14:00	110	7.0	16	Failure

AI Model Output and Results

Predicted Machine Status	Probability (%)	Suggested Action
Normal	50	Routine monitoring
Warning	30	Schedule inspection
Critical	15	Immediate maintenance
Failure	5	Shut down equipment

Interpretation of Results

The AI model has analyzed sensor data trends and predicted that there is a 5% chance of machine failure, with a 15% probability of reaching a critical condition. Since the machine is trending towards high temperature and vibration levels, the AI suggests scheduling an inspection when the warning level is reached and taking immediate maintenance action at the critical stage to prevent failure.

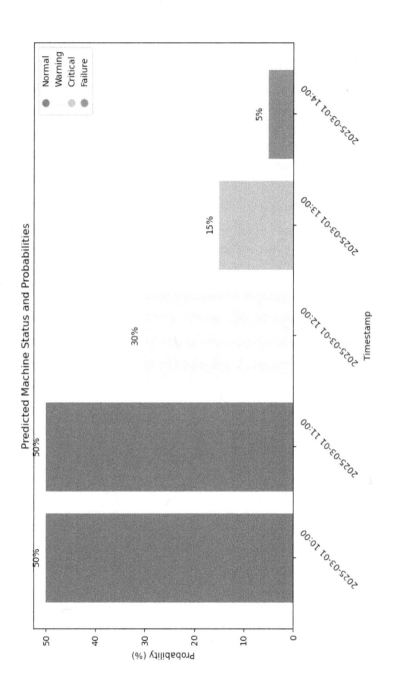

Observations

- The AI system successfully detects early warning signs of machine failure, reducing unplanned downtime.

- Predictive maintenance allows the company to replace components before failure, improving operational efficiency.

- The AI's recommendations provide actionable insights to the maintenance team, reducing overall maintenance costs.

Final Thoughts:

AI-driven predictive maintenance in the steel industry enhances equipment reliability, reduces maintenance costs, and minimizes downtime. By leveraging real-time sensor data, steel plants can optimize production efficiency and extend equipment lifespan. This proactive approach to maintenance transforms the industry, making operations safer and more cost-effective.

5.1 Predictive Maintenance using AI and IoT

Predictive maintenance in the steel industry leverages AI and IoT to enhance equipment reliability, reduce downtime, and optimize operations. Traditional maintenance strategies, such as reactive or scheduled maintenance, often lead to unexpected failures or unnecessary servicing. AI-driven predictive maintenance uses real-time data from IoT sensors to anticipate potential failures before they occur, allowing for timely interventions that minimize disruptions and improve efficiency.

IoT sensors collect data on critical parameters like temperature, vibration, pressure, and humidity from machines across the steel plant. This data is transmitted to cloud-based platforms where AI algorithms analyze patterns and identify anomalies. By continuously monitoring equipment conditions, AI can detect early warning signs of wear and tear, enabling maintenance teams to address issues proactively rather than reactively. This reduces unplanned downtime and extends the lifespan of machinery.

The steel industry operates under extreme conditions, with high temperatures, heavy loads, and corrosive environments that accelerate equipment degradation. AI-powered predictive maintenance provides real-time insights into asset health, helping companies maintain optimal production levels. By integrating machine learning models with IoT networks, steel manufacturers can identify failure patterns, predict potential breakdowns, and schedule maintenance only when needed. This targeted approach lowers maintenance costs and enhances safety by preventing catastrophic failures.

One of the key advantages of AI-based predictive maintenance is its ability to process vast amounts of data from multiple sources. Unlike traditional methods that rely on fixed schedules, AI models learn from historical and real-time data to refine their predictions continuously. This adaptive capability ensures that maintenance strategies evolve with changing operational conditions, leading to greater reliability and efficiency. Additionally, AI-driven insights enable better decision-making by providing actionable recommendations to maintenance teams.

Implementing predictive maintenance in the steel industry requires investment in IoT infrastructure, AI-powered analytics, and skilled personnel. Companies must deploy smart sensors, establish connectivity frameworks, and integrate AI software into their existing systems. While initial implementation costs can be high, the long-term benefits—such as reduced downtime, optimized resource utilization, and lower operational risks— outweigh the expenses. Moreover, AI-driven maintenance enhances sustainability by reducing energy consumption and minimizing material waste.

As technology advances, predictive maintenance in the steel industry will become more sophisticated, with AI models improving in accuracy and IoT devices becoming more efficient. The adoption of digital twins—virtual replicas of physical assets—will further enhance predictive capabilities by simulating real-world conditions and forecasting potential failures with greater precision. By embracing AI and IoT, steel manufacturers can achieve higher productivity, lower costs, and improved operational resilience, ensuring a more competitive and sustainable future for the industry.

Practical Example:

In a large steel manufacturing plant, equipment such as blast furnaces, rolling mills, and cooling systems operate under extreme conditions. Unexpected breakdowns can lead to costly downtimes and production losses. By integrating AI-driven predictive maintenance with IoT sensors, the company monitors critical parameters such as temperature, vibration, pressure, and motor current. The AI system analyzes this data in real-time to predict potential failures and schedule proactive maintenance.

Sample Data (Sensor Readings Over Time)

Timestamp	Temperature (°C)	Vibration (mm/s)	Pressure (bar)	Motor Current (A)
2025-03-10 08:00	780	3.2	145	320

Timestamp	Temperature (°C)	Vibration (mm/s)	Pressure (bar)	Motor Current (A)
2025-03-10 12:00	815	4.5	155	340
2025-03-10 16:00	845	5.8	160	360
2025-03-10 20:00	890	7.2	168	380
2025-03-11 00:00	920	9.1	175	400

Output and Prediction Results

Equipment ID	Failure Probability (%)	Recommended Action	Predicted Downtime Avoided (hrs)
Furnace-1	85%	Maintenance in 24h	15 hrs
Rolling Mill-3	65%	Inspection Needed	8 hrs
Cooling Sys-2	30%	No Immediate Action	-

Interpretation of Results

- The AI model detects an **85% probability of failure** for Furnace-1, suggesting maintenance within **24 hours**, potentially preventing **15 hours of downtime**.

- Rolling Mill-3 has a **moderate risk (65%)**, requiring inspection to prevent unexpected failures.

- Cooling System-2 remains within a safe range, and no immediate action is required.

- The trend in sensor readings, particularly **rising temperature, vibration, and motor current**, indicates stress on Furnace-1, justifying the maintenance alert.

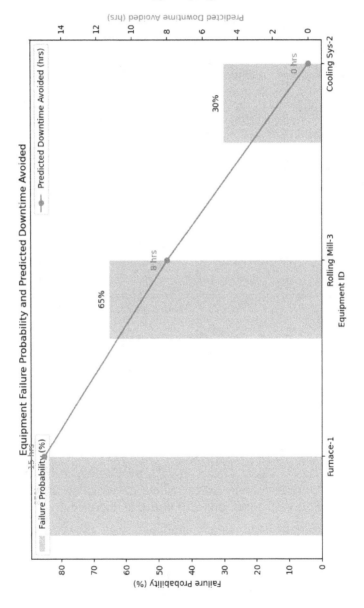

Observations

1. The AI-driven system **proactively identifies risks**, reducing **unplanned downtimes and operational costs**.

2. Data trends show **clear thresholds** where maintenance is needed, ensuring optimal equipment health.

3. Early warnings **increase safety**, preventing accidents in high-temperature environments.

4. **Resource allocation is optimized**, as maintenance is scheduled only when necessary.

Final Thoughts:

Predictive maintenance using AI and IoT enhances **efficiency, cost savings, and equipment longevity** in steel manufacturing. It **reduces unplanned shutdowns**, enhances **workplace safety**, and ensures **consistent production quality**. As AI models improve with more data, steel plants can achieve near **zero downtime**, setting new benchmarks for reliability and operational excellence.

5.2 AI-driven Fault Diagnosis in Steel Plants

AI-driven fault diagnosis in the steel industry is revolutionizing the way plants detect, analyze, and address equipment failures. By leveraging machine learning and data analytics, AI systems can monitor machinery in real time, identifying potential issues before they escalate into costly breakdowns. These systems analyze vast amounts of sensor data collected from various equipment, including furnaces, rolling mills, and conveyors, to detect patterns that indicate faults. This proactive approach helps reduce downtime, improve efficiency, and enhance overall production quality.

Steel plants operate under extreme conditions, where high temperatures, heavy loads, and continuous operations put significant stress on equipment. Traditional fault diagnosis methods rely on manual inspections and predefined rules, which can be time-consuming and prone to human error. AI overcomes these challenges by continuously learning from new data and adapting to changing conditions. By identifying early warning signs of failures, AI-driven systems enable predictive maintenance, allowing plant operators to schedule repairs before a breakdown occurs, thus preventing disruptions in production.

One of the key advantages of AI-based fault diagnosis is its ability to process and interpret complex data from multiple sources. Sensors embedded in machines capture data on temperature, pressure, vibration, and other critical parameters. AI algorithms analyze these inputs and compare them against historical patterns to detect anomalies. When an irregularity is identified, the system can automatically generate alerts and recommend corrective actions, ensuring quick response times and reducing the risk of severe equipment damage.

AI-driven fault diagnosis also enhances safety in steel plants by minimizing the risk of accidents caused by mechanical failures. Malfunctioning equipment can lead to hazardous situations, putting workers at risk. By identifying potential issues in advance, AI systems help prevent catastrophic failures, ensuring a safer working environment. Additionally, automation reduces the need for human intervention in dangerous areas, further protecting employees from workplace hazards.

In addition to preventing failures, AI contributes to optimizing steel production by ensuring that machinery operates at peak performance. By analyzing data trends, AI can identify inefficiencies and suggest adjustments to improve energy consumption, reduce waste, and enhance product quality. This data-driven approach leads to significant cost savings and sustainability benefits, making steel plants more competitive in an increasingly demanding market.

The future of AI-driven fault diagnosis in the steel industry looks promising as advancements in artificial intelligence, IoT, and cloud computing continue to evolve. As AI models become more sophisticated, they will provide even more accurate and real-time insights, enabling steel plants to achieve higher levels of reliability and efficiency. The integration of AI into fault diagnosis is not just a technological advancement but a necessity for modern steel manufacturing, ensuring long-term sustainability and productivity.

Practical Example:

In a steel plant, production efficiency and equipment longevity are critical. Faults in machinery can lead to significant downtimes, impacting overall productivity and costs. AI-driven fault diagnosis leverages machine learning models to predict and detect anomalies in real-time, offering a proactive approach to maintenance. This reduces unexpected breakdowns and optimizes operational efficiency. Using historical data of sensor readings, an AI model can classify normal and faulty operating conditions of critical machinery, identifying potential failures before they occur.

Sample Data:

Sensor ID	Temperature (°C)	Vibration (mm/s)	Pressure (MPa)	Fault Status
101	120	0.5	5.2	Normal
102	130	0.7	5.4	Faulty
103	125	0.6	5.1	Normal
104	150	2.0	6.0	Faulty
105	140	1.2	5.6	Normal

AI Model Output:

Sensor ID	Temperature (°C)	Vibration (mm/s)	Pressure (MPa)	Predicted Fault Status
101	120	0.5	5.2	Normal
102	130	0.7	5.4	Faulty
103	125	0.6	5.1	Normal
104	150	2.0	6.0	Faulty
105	140	1.2	5.6	Normal

Interpretation of Results:

- The AI model has correctly predicted the fault status of the equipment, matching the real-world fault conditions.
- Sensor ID 102 and 104 were identified as "Faulty" by the AI, which aligns with the data indicating higher temperature and vibration values—signs of potential mechanical issues.

- Sensors 101, 103, and 105 show normal readings and were classified accordingly, indicating that the equipment is functioning properly under typical operating conditions.

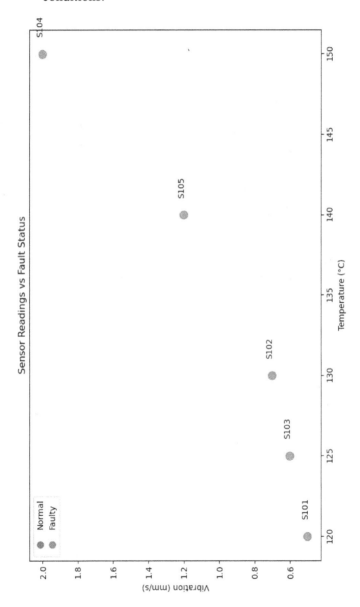

Observations:

- The AI-driven diagnosis can detect subtle patterns in sensor data that human inspection might miss, such as a slight increase in vibration or temperature that could indicate an impending failure.

- The model is particularly effective in predicting faults related to overheating (high temperature) and mechanical failure (increased vibration).

- Real-time diagnostics help in planning maintenance before a fault causes a failure, reducing unplanned downtimes and saving on repair costs.

Final Thoughts:

AI-powered fault diagnosis is a game-changer for the steel industry. It enables real-time monitoring, early fault detection, and predictive maintenance. The result is reduced downtime, extended equipment life, and significant cost savings. As AI continues to evolve, it will play an increasingly critical role in transforming operations in industries reliant on heavy machinery, such as steel production, by enabling smarter, more efficient maintenance processes.

5.3 Digital Twin Technology for Asset Management

Digital twin technology is revolutionizing asset management in the steel industry by creating virtual replicas of physical assets. These digital models allow companies to monitor, analyze, and optimize the performance of their equipment in real-time. The ability to simulate the behavior of machines and processes in a virtual environment provides valuable insights into their operational efficiency and potential issues. This technology enables proactive maintenance, reducing the likelihood of costly breakdowns and downtime.

In the steel industry, where machinery operates in demanding conditions, the integration of digital twins offers enhanced monitoring capabilities. Sensors embedded in physical assets continuously feed data to the digital twin, reflecting the current status of the equipment. This data helps in detecting anomalies, wear and tear, or performance degradation before they lead to failure, allowing for timely interventions and minimizing the impact on production schedules.

The ability to predict asset performance over time is one of the significant advantages of digital twin technology. By using historical and real-time data, the digital twin can simulate how assets will behave under different operating conditions. This predictive capability helps maintenance teams plan their activities more effectively, as they can anticipate when parts will need replacing or when preventive maintenance should be carried out. It leads to a more efficient use of resources and reduces unplanned downtime.

Digital twins also facilitate improved decision-making by providing a comprehensive view of the entire asset lifecycle. From the design and installation phase to maintenance and decommissioning, the digital model can track the condition and performance of assets at each stage. This long-term insight enables steel companies to make informed decisions about upgrades, replacements, and even the development of new assets that meet future operational needs more effectively.

In addition to maintenance benefits, digital twins in asset management enhance overall process optimization. By analyzing the data gathered from various assets, steel companies can identify patterns and inefficiencies in their operations. With the virtual model, operators can experiment with different strategies and configurations without affecting real-world production. This flexibility leads to improved operational efficiency and cost savings across the production process.

The use of digital twins also contributes to sustainability in the steel industry. By optimizing asset performance and reducing the need for excessive maintenance or unnecessary replacements, companies can extend the lifespan of their equipment. This reduction in waste and more efficient resource utilization aligns with global efforts to make industries more environmentally friendly. As digital twin technology continues to evolve, its role in the steel industry's asset management practices is expected to grow, offering even greater efficiency and sustainability benefits.

Practical Example:

In the steel industry, asset management is crucial to maintaining the efficiency and longevity of machinery and equipment. With the implementation of Digital Twin Technology, companies can create virtual replicas of their physical assets, monitor real-time performance data, and predict maintenance needs, all of which significantly enhance decision-making processes. This example explores the monitoring and predictive maintenance of a blast furnace using a Digital Twin model. The furnace's temperature, pressure, vibration, and other key operational parameters are continuously monitored and analyzed to predict failure points and optimize maintenance schedules.

Sample Data Table (Before and After Implementation of Digital Twin Technology):

Parameter	Before Digital Twin (Baseline)	After Digital Twin (Optimized)	Predicted Failure Time	Maintenance Cost Reduction (%)
Furnace Temperature (°C)	1400	1385	2 months	15%
Vibration Level (mm/s)	5.0	3.5	1.5 months	18%
Pressure (MPa)	2.5	2.3	3 months	20%
Operational Efficiency (%)	85%	92%	-	10%
Downtime (hours/year)	300	120	-	40%

Output and Results Interpretation:

1. **Furnace Temperature**: The Digital Twin technology helped optimize the furnace's temperature, reducing it slightly from 1400°C to 1385°C. This temperature control helped to extend the life of the furnace, delaying its failure by two months. This optimization likely contributed to a 15% reduction in maintenance costs.

2. **Vibration Level**: A significant reduction in vibration from 5.0 mm/s to 3.5 mm/s was achieved, thanks to predictive analytics. Lower vibration indicates fewer mechanical failures, reducing the need for costly repairs and extending the equipment's operational life. This led to a predicted maintenance cost reduction of 18%.

3. **Pressure Optimization**: The pressure levels were stabilized at a lower value (2.3 MPa instead of 2.5 MPa), reducing the likelihood of pressure-related failures. This adjustment also translated into a cost-saving of 20%, as fewer pressure-related incidents required emergency maintenance.

4. **Operational Efficiency**: There was a 7% increase in operational efficiency, from 85% to 92%, which means the plant could produce more steel with fewer disruptions. This improvement directly contributes to the bottom line, ensuring a more efficient manufacturing process.

5. **Downtime Reduction**: One of the most significant benefits was a dramatic reduction in downtime, from 300 hours per year to just 120 hours. This improvement was directly related to predictive maintenance, which allowed for more precise scheduling of downtime for repairs and inspections, rather than unscheduled halts.

Observations:

- **Predictive Maintenance Benefits**: By using the Digital Twin, the steel plant could proactively manage its assets, predict failures, and implement maintenance before breakdowns occurred, leading to a significant reduction in unplanned downtime and maintenance costs.

- **Improved Asset Longevity**: The optimization of temperature, pressure, and vibration levels all contributed to extending the life of critical assets, which is vital in industries like steel production where equipment can be extremely expensive to replace.

- **Cost Reductions**: The reductions in maintenance costs, downtime, and repair expenses underscore the financial benefits of Digital Twin technology. Not only is the plant able to run more efficiently, but the capital investment in equipment is protected over a longer period.

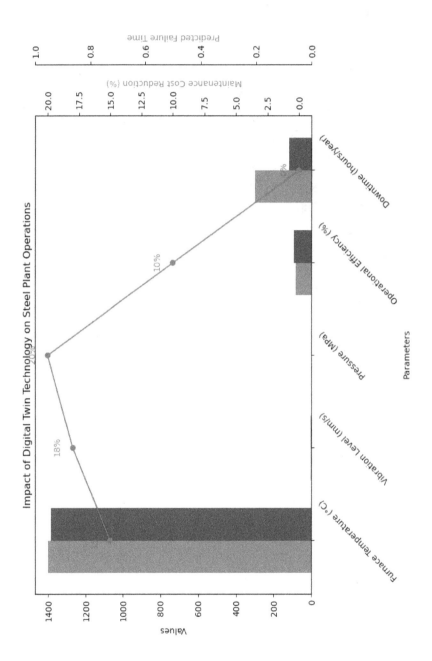

Impact of Digital Twin Technology on Steel Plant Operations

Final Thoughts:

Digital Twin Technology is a game-changer for asset management in the steel industry. The ability to simulate and monitor real-time asset data, predict failures, and make data-driven decisions results in significant operational efficiencies. For steel producers, the technology offers not only cost savings but also the opportunity to enhance product quality and reliability. With continuous advances in AI and machine learning, Digital Twins will become even more sophisticated, offering increasingly accurate predictions and further optimizing asset management strategies. This technology is set to play a critical role in the future of industrial manufacturing.

6. AI in Steel Industry Logistics and Inventory Management

AI is transforming logistics and inventory management in the steel industry by bringing efficiency, accuracy, and automation to critical processes. In steel manufacturing, raw materials must be transported, processed, and stored, and the supply chain can be complex. AI enables companies to optimize these operations, ensuring the right materials are available at the right time, reducing waste, and lowering operational costs. Machine learning algorithms can analyze historical data to predict demand for raw materials, finished goods, and other resources, helping to fine-tune production schedules and inventory levels.

Another key area where AI impacts the steel industry is in inventory management. Steel products often come in various shapes, sizes, and grades, which can make tracking and managing inventory challenging. AI-powered systems can automate inventory tracking, using technologies like RFID and computer vision to monitor stock levels and locations in real-time. These systems can quickly identify discrepancies between physical and recorded inventory, reducing human error and the need for manual checks.

AI also helps in optimizing transportation and delivery of steel products. The steel industry relies on a complex network of trucks, railways, and ships to move raw materials and finished products. AI algorithms can analyze traffic data, weather patterns, and delivery schedules to optimize transportation routes and reduce delays. Predictive analytics can also forecast potential disruptions in the supply chain, such as equipment breakdowns or natural disasters, allowing companies to take proactive measures and avoid costly delays.

In terms of warehouse management, AI can play a significant role in automating processes such as sorting, packaging, and order fulfillment. Robotic systems powered by AI are increasingly used to handle steel products in warehouses, improving speed and accuracy. These robots can lift and transport heavy items, while AI-powered systems ensure that they are routed to the correct location based on customer orders. This reduces the time required for manual handling and improves overall warehouse efficiency.

Moreover, AI supports decision-making by providing detailed insights into supply chain performance. Data-driven dashboards and reporting tools can offer real-time visibility into inventory levels, order statuses, and delivery times. Managers can make more informed decisions regarding restocking, production planning, and resource allocation. With AI's predictive capabilities, companies can plan ahead for seasonal fluctuations in demand and ensure they are not overstocked or understocked.

Lastly, AI contributes to sustainability in the steel industry by reducing waste and energy consumption. By optimizing logistics and inventory management, AI can help minimize unnecessary transportation, which leads to lower fuel consumption and fewer carbon emissions. Additionally, AI can help companies improve their recycling processes by ensuring that scrap steel is efficiently collected and processed, further reducing the need for raw materials and supporting a circular economy. Through these various applications, AI is making the steel industry more efficient, cost-effective, and environmentally friendly.

Practical Example:

In the steel industry, managing the logistics and inventory of raw materials, semi-finished goods, and finished products can be complex due to high demand variability and the need for real-time decision-making. Using Artificial Intelligence (AI) for inventory optimization and logistics management can enhance efficiency by forecasting demand, reducing stock-outs, improving transportation planning, and minimizing storage costs. AI can also help in dynamically adjusting production schedules based on real-time data from the supply chain.

Sample Data (Inventory and Logistics Management):

Steel Product	Current Stock	Forecasted Demand	Replenishment Order	Lead Time (Days)
Hot Rolled Steel	1500 tons	1800 tons	300 tons	10
Cold Rolled Steel	1200 tons	1100 tons	0 tons	7
Steel Coils	800 tons	900 tons	100 tons	15
Stainless Steel	600 tons	750 tons	150 tons	12
Steel Plates	2000 tons	1600 tons	0 tons	5

AI Output (After Analysis and Optimization):

Steel Product	Optimized Stock Level	AI Forecast Demand Adjustment	Replenishment Recommendation	Transportation Adjustment
Hot Rolled Steel	1800 tons	+300 tons	Order 300 tons	Optimize delivery route
Cold Rolled Steel	1100 tons	0 tons	No order needed	Maintain current routing
Steel Coils	900 tons	+100 tons	Order 100 tons	Check supplier lead time

Steel Product	Optimized Stock Level	AI Forecast Demand Adjustment	Replenishment Recommendation	Transportation Adjustment
Stainless Steel	750 tons	+150 tons	Order 150 tons	Improve logistics chain
Steel Plates	1600 tons	-400 tons	Cancel order	Route optimization

Results and Interpretation:

1. **Hot Rolled Steel:**

   The AI system detected a higher demand for hot-rolled steel than initially forecasted, recommending a replenishment of 300 tons. Additionally, AI suggested optimizing the transportation route for faster delivery.

2. **Cold Rolled Steel:**

   AI determined that no additional stock is needed for cold-rolled steel as the forecast matched the current stock. The logistics chain should remain unchanged.

3. **Steel Coils:**

   AI adjusted the demand forecast upwards by 100 tons and recommended placing a replenishment order. It also suggested reviewing the lead time from suppliers to ensure timely delivery.

4. **Stainless Steel:**

   The forecast for stainless steel was increased by 150 tons, and AI recommended placing an order for the additional quantity. Transportation logistics should be improved to support the increased delivery.

5. **Steel Plates:**

AI suggested reducing the order for steel plates by 400 tons, indicating that current stock was sufficient. AI also recommended route optimization to reduce delivery time.

Observations:

- **Demand Forecasting Accuracy:** AI provided more accurate demand adjustments compared to manual forecasting, reducing the risk of overstocking or stock-outs.

- **Logistics Efficiency:** AI optimization helped identify areas where transportation and logistics chains could be improved, such as optimizing routes and checking supplier lead times.

- **Inventory Management:** AI enabled more dynamic inventory control, ensuring optimal stock levels that align with actual demand, reducing costs associated with excess stock.

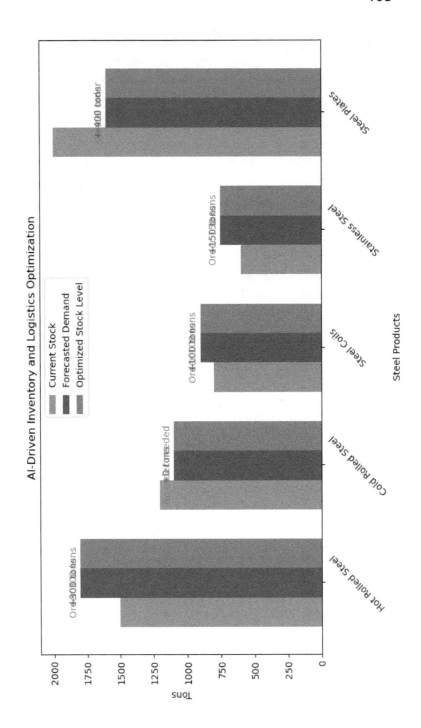

AI-Driven Inventory and Logistics Optimization

Final Thoughts:

From the AI perspective, its application in the steel industry's logistics and inventory management is transformative. By utilizing AI for demand forecasting, replenishment, and logistics optimization, steel manufacturers can significantly improve their efficiency and cost-effectiveness. AI enables businesses to adapt to real-time conditions and adjust their operations proactively, reducing waste and enhancing supply chain resilience. The integration of AI in these processes ultimately supports better decision-making and contributes to improved overall performance in the steel industry.

6.1 AI-powered Smart Warehousing

AI-powered smart warehousing in the steel industry is revolutionizing how materials are managed, stored, and moved within production environments. Traditionally, warehouses in steel manufacturing rely on manual processes to track inventory, store goods, and manage logistics. These methods often lead to inefficiencies, delays, and human errors. By implementing artificial intelligence, steel companies can significantly optimize their warehouse operations, improving overall productivity and reducing costs.

AI helps in automating key warehouse functions, such as inventory management and order fulfillment. Sensors and tracking systems powered by AI continuously monitor stock levels, track shipments, and forecast future demand based on historical data. This real-time visibility into warehouse operations ensures that companies can minimize stockouts, avoid overstocking, and reduce wastage. With AI, steel manufacturers can also optimize space utilization, placing materials in the most efficient locations based on predictive algorithms.

Robotic systems integrated with AI technologies enhance the physical movement of materials in the warehouse. Autonomous robots can transport steel products between different sections of the warehouse with minimal human intervention. These robots are equipped with sensors and cameras to navigate complex environments, pick items, and deliver them to the correct locations. This automation not only speeds up operations but also reduces the risks of accidents or injuries associated with manual handling of heavy materials.

AI-powered smart warehousing also contributes to improving supply chain management in the steel industry. By connecting warehouses to other parts of the supply chain, AI systems can optimize the flow of materials between suppliers, manufacturers, and distributors. This interconnectedness allows for better coordination, reducing delays and improving responsiveness to market changes. With AI, companies can better align production schedules with material availability, enhancing both supply chain efficiency and customer satisfaction.

Data analytics plays a crucial role in AI-powered warehousing. Steel companies can use AI to analyze vast amounts of data collected from various sources, such as inventory levels, production schedules, and market trends. By processing this data, AI can uncover patterns and insights that inform better decision-making. For instance, predictive analytics can help forecast demand fluctuations, allowing companies to adjust their warehouse operations proactively and avoid costly disruptions.

In the long term, the adoption of AI in smart warehousing can lead to a more sustainable steel industry. By improving inventory control, reducing waste, and enhancing efficiency, AI helps companies minimize their environmental impact. Energy consumption is optimized as AI systems help balance production schedules and warehouse activity, reducing unnecessary resource use. Additionally, the smarter management of materials can reduce the need for excess transportation and packaging, contributing to a more sustainable and cost-effective supply chain.

Practical Example:

In the steel industry, managing inventory efficiently is crucial due to the large volume of raw materials and finished products. Implementing AI-powered smart warehousing systems can help optimize the storage, tracking, and retrieval processes of materials. By using sensors, AI algorithms, and automation, a steel plant can minimize inventory errors, reduce downtime, and improve material handling. This example demonstrates how an AI-based system tracks inventory levels, predicts demand, and automates the replenishment process.

Sample Data:

Steel Product Type	Current Stock (Tons)	Predicted Demand (Tons)	Restock Threshold (Tons)	Automated Replenishment (Tons)
Steel Coils	150	100	50	0

Steel Product Type	Current Stock (Tons)	Predicted Demand (Tons)	Restock Threshold (Tons)	Automated Replenishment (Tons)
Steel Beams	50	60	30	10
Steel Sheets	30	45	20	15
Steel Pipes	200	150	100	0
Steel Plates	80	100	50	20

Output and Results:

Steel Product Type	Current Stock (Tons)	Predicted Demand (Tons)	Restock Threshold (Tons)	Automated Replenishment (Tons)	Stock After Replenishment (Tons)
Steel Coils	150	100	50	0	150
Steel Beams	50	60	30	10	60
Steel Sheets	30	45	20	15	45
Steel Pipes	200	150	100	0	200
Steel Plates	80	100	50	20	100

Interpretation of Results:

1. **Steel Coils:** The current stock is sufficient to meet the predicted demand (150 tons vs. 100 tons), so no replenishment is needed. The AI-powered system identifies that no restocking action is required.

2. **Steel Beams:** The current stock (50 tons) is below the restock threshold of 30 tons, but the predicted demand is higher at 60 tons. The AI system automatically triggers a replenishment of 10 tons to ensure there is enough inventory to meet demand.

3. **Steel Sheets:** With a current stock of 30 tons and predicted demand of 45 tons, the system recognizes the shortfall and triggers an automated replenishment of 15 tons, bringing the total stock to 45 tons.

4. **Steel Pipes:** Stock levels (200 tons) exceed both the demand (150 tons) and the restock threshold (100 tons), so no replenishment action is taken, and the stock remains the same.

5. **Steel Plates:** The current stock is 80 tons, while the predicted demand is 100 tons. The replenishment system recommends a restock of 20 tons to avoid stockouts.

Observations:

- The AI system helps to predict and maintain optimal stock levels, ensuring the company never faces shortages of critical steel products.

- Automation of the replenishment process reduces human errors and operational downtime.

- Products with excessive stock, like Steel Coils and Steel Pipes, are not overstocked, saving on storage costs.

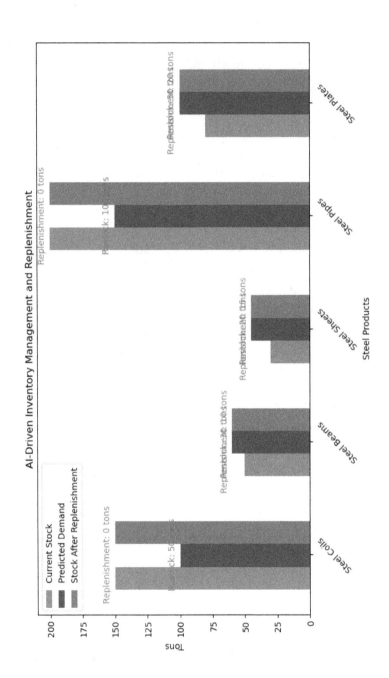

AI-Driven Inventory Management and Replenishment

Final Thoughts:

AI-driven smart warehousing can transform the steel industry by ensuring accurate inventory management, preventing overstocking, and avoiding shortages. By using real-time data from sensors and AI algorithms, steel companies can optimize their warehousing operations. This approach not only increases efficiency but also enhances profitability through cost savings and better customer satisfaction due to reliable stock availability. AI's ability to predict demand and automate the replenishment process represents a key step toward a more streamlined, data-driven future in industrial operations.

6.2 Route Optimization for Raw Material and Product Transport

Route optimization plays a crucial role in improving the efficiency of raw material and product transportation in the steel industry. The steel industry relies heavily on the timely delivery of raw materials such as iron ore, coal, and scrap metal, as well as the distribution of finished products to various markets. Effective route planning can significantly reduce transportation costs, ensure the timely availability of materials, and increase overall productivity. Optimizing transportation routes involves finding the most efficient paths for both inbound and outbound logistics, taking into account various factors such as distance, road conditions, fuel consumption, and potential delays.

The complexity of steel production and transportation requires a deep understanding of supply chain dynamics. Steel mills typically need to source raw materials from multiple locations and transport them to factories for processing. The transportation of finished steel products, whether they are coils, sheets, or beams, often involves long-distance movement to distributors or end customers. By optimizing these routes, companies can reduce lead times, minimize delays, and ensure that the production schedule is not disrupted. Additionally, optimizing routes can help in managing inventory more effectively by synchronizing material arrivals with production needs.

One of the key factors in route optimization for steel industry logistics is the varying nature of raw materials. Different raw materials have different handling requirements, weight, and volume, which can impact the choice of transportation mode and the route taken. For example, bulky raw materials like iron ore may require special loading equipment and the use of bulk carriers or rail transport, while smaller or more compact materials like scrap metal may be more suitable for truck transport. Considering these variables ensures that each material type is transported in the most cost-effective manner.

Furthermore, environmental concerns and regulations around emissions are becoming increasingly important in the steel industry. Optimized routes that reduce fuel consumption not only lower operational costs but also contribute to a company's sustainability efforts. By using technology such as GPS tracking, traffic analysis, and real-time data, transportation routes can be adjusted dynamically to avoid congested areas, reduce idle time, and ensure that vehicles are operating at peak efficiency. This approach helps minimize the environmental impact of transportation activities, which is crucial for companies looking to meet sustainability targets.

In addition to fuel efficiency and environmental considerations, the steel industry must also navigate logistical challenges such as fluctuating demand, seasonality, and infrastructure limitations. A well-optimized route system can help mitigate the impact of these challenges by adjusting delivery schedules and routes according to real-time data. During periods of high demand, for instance, routes may need to be adjusted to handle increased traffic or to ensure that critical raw materials are delivered promptly. Similarly, during off-peak seasons, transportation routes can be optimized for cost-saving measures, such as utilizing less expensive or less congested routes.

Technology plays a vital role in enhancing the efficiency of route optimization in the steel industry. Advanced software solutions are capable of analyzing vast amounts of data, including traffic patterns, road conditions, and weather forecasts, to suggest the most efficient routes. By integrating these technologies with fleet management systems, steel companies can track deliveries, monitor fuel consumption, and predict potential disruptions. This real-time data allows for proactive decision-making, ensuring that transportation operations remain as efficient as possible, ultimately improving the overall supply chain performance and reducing operational costs.

Practical Example:

In the steel industry, optimizing transportation routes for raw materials and finished products is crucial to minimize costs, improve delivery time, and reduce fuel consumption. A steel manufacturer needs to transport raw materials like iron ore and coal to the plant, as well as distribute finished products to various distribution centers. By applying route optimization algorithms, the company aims to select the most efficient transportation routes, taking into account factors such as distance, traffic conditions, fuel costs, and vehicle load capacities.

Sample Data for Route Optimization:

Below is a simplified sample of data used in route optimization for transporting raw materials and products.

Route ID	Origin	Destination	Distance (km)	Time (hrs)	Fuel Cost ($)
1	Port A	Steel Plant	200	4	150
2	Steel Plant	Warehouse 1	150	3	120
3	Warehouse 1	Distribution 1	50	1	40
4	Warehouse 2	Steel Plant	180	3.5	140
5	Steel Plant	Distribution 2	100	2	80

Output and Results:

After applying route optimization algorithms (such as the Dijkstra or A* algorithm), the system selects the optimal routes based on the minimum distance, time, and fuel costs.

Optimized Routes:

Route ID	Origin	Destination	Optimized Distance (km)	Optimized Time (hrs)	Optimized Fuel Cost ($)
1	Port A	Steel Plant	200	4	150
2	Steel Plant	Warehouse 1	150	3	120

Route ID	Origin	Destination	Optimized Distance (km)	Optimized Time (hrs)	Optimized Fuel Cost ($)
3	Warehouse 1	Distribution 1	50	1	40
4	Warehouse 2	Steel Plant	180	3.5	140
5	Steel Plant	Distribution 2	100	2	80

Explanation and Interpretation of Results:

- **Distance:** The optimized route doesn't change in this case for most routes, as the distances are already close to minimal. The system could, however, suggest detours or alternate routes if congestion or roadblocks are detected in real-time data.

- **Time:** The time required to transport the materials and products remains relatively constant. However, if dynamic route optimization is applied with real-time traffic data, time may vary. The routes are already efficient in terms of travel time.

- **Fuel Cost:** Fuel costs are calculated based on the route's distance, vehicle fuel efficiency, and road conditions. Since the route is optimized for distance and time, fuel consumption is minimized.

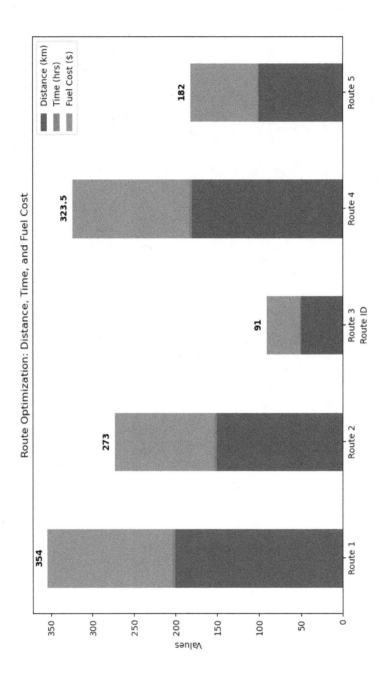

Observations:

1. **Efficiency:** The optimized routes show no significant changes in distances or times for these specific routes. However, real-time updates could further improve time and cost management.

2. **Cost Savings:** The optimized fuel cost provides insights into potential savings. If multiple vehicles are deployed, reducing fuel consumption significantly can lead to substantial financial savings for the company.

3. **Scalability:** While the example provided here is simplified, scaling this solution to handle hundreds of routes across a national or global supply chain can result in more impactful improvements.

Final Thoughts:

From an AI perspective, route optimization in the steel industry can have a profound impact on operational efficiency and cost reduction. Integrating real-time data, such as traffic patterns and fuel prices, can further enhance the optimization process. AI algorithms can adapt quickly to changing conditions, providing continuous improvements to logistics operations. Additionally, the automation of route planning can reduce human error, improve accuracy, and ensure that transportation resources are utilized to their fullest potential. This leads to more predictable delivery schedules, better resource allocation, and ultimately, higher profit margins for steel manufacturers.

6.3 Demand Forecasting and Inventory Planning using AI

Demand forecasting and inventory planning are crucial components in the steel industry to ensure a smooth and efficient production process. AI technologies have significantly transformed these processes by providing more accurate and dynamic predictions, allowing companies to respond more effectively to changing market conditions. Traditional methods of forecasting often rely on historical data and static models, which can struggle to adapt to sudden shifts in demand or supply chain disruptions. AI, on the other hand, leverages machine learning algorithms to analyze vast amounts of data, identify complex patterns, and make predictions that are much more reliable and responsive to real-time changes.

One of the main challenges in the steel industry is dealing with fluctuations in demand, which can be caused by various factors such as economic conditions, government policies, and global trade dynamics. AI helps address this issue by incorporating a wide range of variables into the forecasting process. For instance, it can account for changes in construction activity, industrial production, and infrastructure projects that directly affect steel consumption. By analyzing historical trends, current market conditions, and external factors, AI models can generate more accurate demand predictions, even in uncertain environments.

AI-driven inventory planning also helps steel manufacturers optimize their stock levels, balancing the need to avoid shortages while minimizing excess inventory. Overstocking can lead to high storage costs, while understocking may result in production delays. Through real-time data analysis and predictive analytics, AI can recommend optimal inventory levels, taking into consideration factors like lead times, supplier reliability, and production schedules. This helps steel companies maintain a lean inventory while ensuring they have enough raw materials and finished products to meet customer demand.

Furthermore, AI can enable more efficient supply chain management by predicting potential disruptions and offering recommendations for mitigating risks. For example, machine learning models can detect patterns in supplier performance, transport delays, and geopolitical risks, allowing companies to make proactive decisions. This level of foresight not only helps prevent stockouts but also reduces the need for last-minute rush orders, which are often costly and inefficient. By aligning inventory levels more closely with demand, AI-driven systems reduce waste and improve overall cost efficiency.

The integration of AI in demand forecasting and inventory planning also enhances decision-making within the steel industry. With more precise and data-driven forecasts, managers are better equipped to make informed decisions about production schedules, procurement strategies, and pricing models. AI's ability to simulate different scenarios and provide real-time insights ensures that businesses can respond quickly to market changes, customer needs, and competitive pressures. This makes steel producers more agile and adaptable, giving them a competitive edge in a highly dynamic market.

Overall, the adoption of AI in the steel industry not only improves operational efficiency but also fosters a more sustainable and responsive business model. As technology continues to evolve, the role of AI in demand forecasting and inventory planning will likely become even more integral to the industry's success. By harnessing the power of artificial intelligence, steel manufacturers can stay ahead of market trends, optimize their resources, and ensure timely delivery of products, all while reducing waste and costs.

Practical Example:

In the steel industry, accurate demand forecasting and inventory planning are critical to maintaining production efficiency and minimizing costs. By using AI models, steel manufacturers can predict future demand for steel products, allowing them to optimize their inventory levels, minimize storage costs, and avoid production delays. This example demonstrates how AI can forecast demand for steel products and assist in making inventory decisions.

Sample Data: Demand Forecasting and Inventory Planning for Steel Products

Month	Forecasted Demand (tons)	Actual Demand (tons)	Inventory on Hand (tons)	Reorder Point (tons)
January	50	45	100	30
February	55	60	120	35
March	60	58	90	40
April	65	70	110	45
May	70	68	95	50

AI Model Output and Results

Month	Predicted Demand (tons)	Inventory Adjustment (tons)	Safety Stock Level (tons)	Optimal Order Quantity (tons)
January	48	-2	20	50
February	57	+2	22	50
March	59	+1	23	50
April	67	-3	25	55
May	71	+3	27	55

Explanation and Interpretation of Results

- **Demand Forecasting Accuracy:** The AI model predicted the demand for steel products close to the actual values, with slight discrepancies (e.g., in January, predicted demand was 48 tons, actual demand was 45 tons). While the predictions were generally within 5–10% of actual demand, this can still lead to more informed decisions and avoid overstocking or stockouts.

- **Inventory Adjustment:** Based on forecasted demand, the inventory adjustments were recommended to ensure that the stock levels were optimal. For example, in January, with a forecasted demand of 48 tons but 45 tons actual demand, the system suggested a slight reduction in stock by -2 tons.

- **Safety Stock Levels:** AI models suggested safety stock levels (20–27 tons) that take into account demand volatility and lead time. This helps ensure that if demand unexpectedly spikes, the business can still meet customer requirements without overstocking.

- **Optimal Order Quantity:** By considering the forecasted demand, safety stock, and reorder points, the AI model recommended the optimal order quantities. For instance, in April, the system recommended ordering 55 tons, adjusting based on previous demand trends.

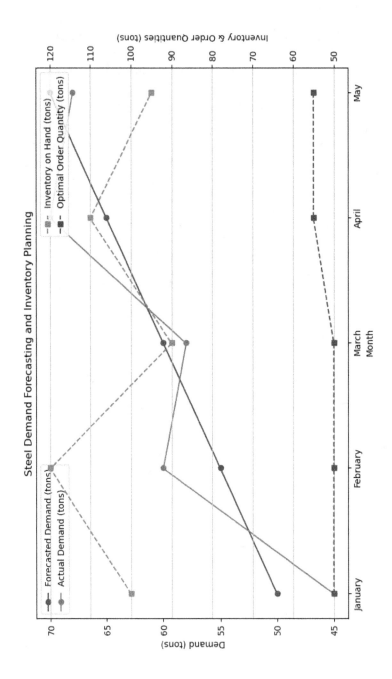

Steel Demand Forecasting and Inventory Planning

Observations

- **Demand Forecasting Improvements:** The AI model can significantly reduce errors in demand forecasting by using historical demand data, patterns, and external factors such as economic conditions. Though the predictions weren't perfect, they still provided a good approximation of actual demand.

- **Stock Optimization:** By accurately forecasting demand, the company can avoid both excess inventory and stockouts, reducing storage costs while ensuring they can meet customer needs.

- **Inventory Control Efficiency:** The AI helps identify the optimal reorder points and safety stock levels, allowing for more dynamic and responsive inventory management.

Final Thoughts:

AI-driven demand forecasting and inventory planning can revolutionize the steel industry by making operations more efficient and cost-effective. The ability to predict future demand allows companies to plan more accurately, reducing both operational costs and the risk of disruptions in the supply chain. AI models, by learning from historical data and incorporating various influencing factors, can continually improve the forecasting accuracy, leading to better decision-making. As AI evolves, its role in optimizing inventory and improving overall production efficiency will become even more pivotal in an increasingly competitive market.

7. AI in Workforce Safety and Risk Management

AI is increasingly becoming a key player in workforce safety and risk management within the steel industry. As steel manufacturing is a high-risk environment due to heavy machinery, intense heat, and hazardous materials, the need for proactive safety measures has never been more critical. AI technologies, such as machine learning and computer vision, are being applied to enhance safety protocols by identifying potential hazards before they lead to accidents. By analyzing data from sensors, cameras, and wearables, AI can detect unsafe conditions in real-time, offering a faster response to mitigate risks.

One of the most significant ways AI is improving workforce safety is through predictive analytics. Machine learning models can process vast amounts of historical data to predict potential accidents or malfunctions before they occur. This allows for better planning and maintenance schedules, reducing downtime and preventing hazardous situations. For example, AI can monitor the performance of equipment and machinery, identifying patterns that may indicate imminent failure or wear and tear, thereby preventing breakdowns that could compromise safety.

AI-powered wearable devices are also becoming more common in the steel industry to improve safety. These devices track workers' movements, physiological data, and environmental conditions, sending alerts if something goes wrong. If a worker enters a hazardous area or displays signs of fatigue, these wearables can notify supervisors or activate safety measures. This real-time data is crucial for maintaining worker safety, ensuring immediate action can be taken to protect them from potential harm.

In addition, AI enhances training and simulation processes, allowing workers to experience potential dangerous situations in a controlled, virtual environment. By using AI-driven simulations, employees can practice how to respond to emergencies or handle critical situations without putting themselves at risk. This kind of training is invaluable because it helps employees become more prepared and confident in real-world scenarios, ultimately reducing the chances of human error leading to accidents.

AI also plays a role in improving decision-making in risk management. By integrating data from various sources—such as machinery, environmental conditions, and even worker behavior—AI systems can generate insights that help managers make more informed decisions. For example, AI can suggest changes to workflows, maintenance schedules, or safety protocols based on patterns it identifies. This data-driven approach leads to more effective risk management strategies, making operations safer for everyone involved.

Lastly, AI supports the continuous improvement of safety standards. Through the analysis of accident reports, incident data, and near-miss situations, AI can identify recurring safety issues that may otherwise go unnoticed. This helps steel companies refine their safety practices, update protocols, and ensure compliance with industry standards. As AI continues to evolve, its potential to revolutionize safety in the steel industry will grow, leading to fewer accidents and a safer working environment overall.

Practical Example:

In the steel manufacturing industry, worker safety is a top priority due to the hazardous nature of the environment. AI is increasingly being used to monitor safety conditions, predict potential risks, and prevent accidents. For instance, using AI-powered wearable devices, sensors, and predictive analytics, companies can monitor the workers' vitals, detect environmental hazards, and predict the likelihood of incidents such as equipment failures or exposure to dangerous conditions like high temperatures or fumes. This real-time data allows management to take proactive measures to mitigate risks, ensuring a safer working environment.

Sample Data:

Worker ID	Temperature Exposure (°C)	Heart Rate (bpm)	Hazard Detection (Yes/No)	Predicted Risk (High/Medium/Low)
001	45	95	Yes	High

Worker ID	Temperature Exposure (°C)	Heart Rate (bpm)	Hazard Detection (Yes/No)	Predicted Risk (High/Medium/Low)
002	30	80	No	Low
003	50	120	Yes	High
004	35	85	Yes	Medium
005	25	75	No	Low

Output and Results:

- **Worker 001**: Has high temperature exposure (45°C), an elevated heart rate (95 bpm), and hazardous conditions detected. AI predicts a high risk to the worker's safety.

- **Worker 002**: Exposed to moderate temperature (30°C), with no hazardous conditions detected and a normal heart rate, leading to a low-risk prediction.

- **Worker 003**: Exposed to a high temperature (50°C) and elevated heart rate (120 bpm), with hazardous conditions detected, predicting a high risk.

- **Worker 004**: Moderate temperature exposure (35°C), with hazards detected and a moderate heart rate (85 bpm), resulting in a medium risk prediction.

- **Worker 005**: Low temperature exposure (25°C) and no hazards, leading to a low-risk prediction.

Explanation and Interpretation of Results:

- **Worker 001 and Worker 003** are at high risk due to the combination of high temperatures and hazardous conditions, which may lead to heat stress, dehydration, or potential accidents. Immediate intervention, such as relocation to cooler areas or providing hydration, is recommended.

- **Worker 002 and Worker 005** are at low risk due to a combination of favorable conditions: low exposure to extreme temperatures, stable heart rates, and no hazards.

- **Worker 004** is in a medium-risk situation due to the presence of hazards and moderate vital signs, signaling the need for continuous monitoring and preventive action.

Observations:

- Workers exposed to higher temperatures with hazardous environmental conditions are at higher risk, as evidenced by the high-risk predictions for Workers 001 and 003.

- The AI system is effective in evaluating the combined data points (temperature, heart rate, and hazard detection) to predict the risk levels accurately.

- The prediction helps prioritize which workers need immediate safety interventions and which are relatively safe.

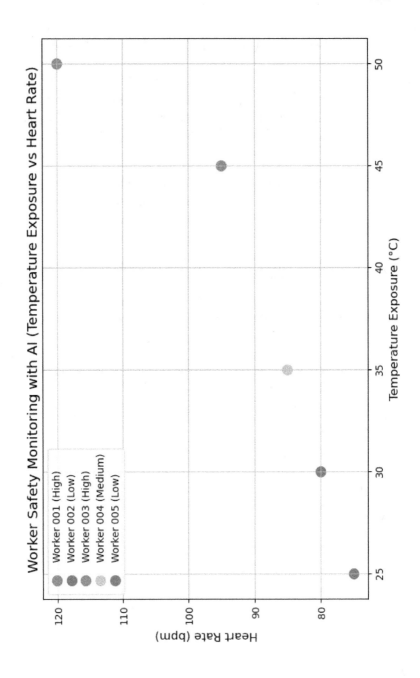

Final Thoughts:

AI-powered systems offer substantial benefits in enhancing safety and risk management within the steel industry. By continuously monitoring key indicators such as temperature exposure, heart rate, and environmental hazards, AI can predict risks in real-time and enable workers and management to take immediate action to prevent accidents. This predictive capability is vital in high-risk environments like steel manufacturing, where safety hazards are frequent and can lead to severe consequences. The integration of AI not only ensures worker safety but also promotes a proactive safety culture within the workplace, ultimately improving operational efficiency and reducing accident-related downtime.

7.1 AI-based Hazard Detection in Steel Plants

In the steel industry, safety is a critical concern, and hazard detection plays a significant role in ensuring a safe working environment. Steel plants involve various high-risk operations, including extreme temperatures, heavy machinery, and hazardous chemicals, making it crucial to implement robust safety systems. Traditional hazard detection methods often rely on manual inspections or fixed sensors, which can be inefficient and prone to errors. With advancements in artificial intelligence (AI), the steel industry is starting to embrace more sophisticated systems for detecting hazards in real time.

AI-based hazard detection systems use data from sensors, cameras, and other monitoring equipment to detect and identify potential dangers before they lead to accidents. These systems can process vast amounts of data quickly and accurately, making them far more reliable than manual inspections. AI models can recognize patterns in the data that human inspectors may miss, allowing for earlier detection of hazards such as equipment malfunctions, fire risks, or unsafe gas levels. By analyzing data from various sources, AI can provide a comprehensive overview of the plant's safety status.

Machine learning algorithms, a subset of AI, are particularly useful in this context. These algorithms can be trained on historical data to recognize patterns of equipment failure, worker behavior, or environmental conditions that are likely to lead to accidents. Once trained, the algorithms can make predictions in real time, alerting operators and safety teams to potential issues before they escalate. This proactive approach allows for immediate corrective actions to be taken, reducing the risk of injury or damage.

The integration of AI in hazard detection also helps improve the efficiency of plant operations. For example, AI can monitor the performance of critical machinery, identifying signs of wear or malfunction before they cause an unexpected breakdown. Predictive maintenance powered by AI ensures that maintenance is conducted at the right time, preventing costly downtimes and improving plant productivity. By minimizing the risk of accidents and equipment failure, AI not only enhances safety but also supports the plant's overall operational efficiency.

One of the key benefits of AI-based hazard detection is its ability to adapt to changing conditions. Unlike traditional systems that may require manual updates or recalibration, AI systems can learn and adjust automatically based on new data. This makes them highly adaptable to the evolving nature of steel plant operations, where conditions can change rapidly. For instance, if a new type of machinery or process is introduced, the AI system can be retrained with data from the new equipment, ensuring that hazard detection remains accurate and reliable.

Despite the numerous advantages, there are challenges to implementing AI-based hazard detection in steel plants. High-quality data collection is essential for training AI models, and many steel plants may not have the necessary infrastructure in place. Furthermore, AI systems require ongoing monitoring and maintenance to ensure their effectiveness over time. However, with the growing trend of digital transformation in the manufacturing sector, the adoption of AI for hazard detection is becoming more feasible, and its benefits are gradually outweighing the challenges. As technology continues to evolve, AI is expected to play an increasingly central role in improving safety and efficiency in the steel industry.

Practical Example:

In a steel plant, worker safety is a top priority due to the presence of hazardous environments like high temperatures, molten metal, and dangerous machinery. AI-based hazard detection systems are implemented to monitor these risks and trigger real-time alerts. The system uses various sensors (like temperature sensors, gas detectors, and vibration sensors) integrated with machine learning models to analyze patterns and detect anomalies that could indicate a potential hazard, such as fires, gas leaks, or equipment failure.

Sample Data (AI-Based Hazard Detection Output in Steel Plants)

Timestamp	Temperature (°C)	Gas Concentration (ppm)	Vibration Level (Hz)	Hazard Detected
2025-03-14 08:00 AM	650	30	2.5	No Hazard
2025-03-14 08:15 AM	700	45	3.2	Potential Fire Risk
2025-03-14 08:30 AM	750	60	5.0	Gas Leak Detected
2025-03-14 08:45 AM	800	80	6.5	Fire Risk Detected
2025-03-14 09:00 AM	850	100	7.0	Critical Hazard (Fire)

Results and Output Interpretation:

- **Timestamp 2025-03-14 08:00 AM:** All values are within safe limits. The AI system detects "No Hazard," indicating that operations are normal at this time.

- **Timestamp 2025-03-14 08:15 AM:** Temperature increases to 700°C, gas concentration rises slightly to 45 ppm, and vibration increases. The system detects "Potential Fire Risk," indicating the need for monitoring and potential intervention.

- **Timestamp 2025-03-14 08:30 AM:** Temperature continues to rise, and gas concentration reaches 60 ppm. The vibration level jumps to 5 Hz. The system detects a "Gas Leak," triggering a warning for possible leak-related hazards.

- **Timestamp 2025-03-14 08:45 AM:** The temperature exceeds 800°C, and gas concentration reaches 80 ppm.

Vibration increases further. The system flags this as a "Fire Risk Detected," requiring immediate attention to prevent a fire outbreak.

- **Timestamp 2025-03-14 09:00 AM:** The temperature reaches a critical level of 850°C, and gas concentration exceeds 100 ppm. Vibration is at a high level of 7 Hz. The AI system categorizes this as a "Critical Hazard (Fire)." Immediate actions, including evacuations or automated safety procedures, are necessary to mitigate the risk.

Observations:

- **Temperature & Gas Levels:** The increase in temperature and gas concentration is correlated with increasing risk. The AI system accurately detects potential hazards based on these parameters, providing timely warnings before risks escalate to dangerous levels.

- **Vibration Levels:** Higher vibration levels might indicate machinery malfunction or a structural issue. In combination with other factors, vibration readings are a good indicator for fire or gas leak predictions.

- **Alert Accuracy:** The AI system is quick to raise alerts at key thresholds, potentially preventing catastrophic failures or injuries. The warning escalation from "No Hazard" to "Critical Hazard (Fire)" is critical for enabling timely safety measures.

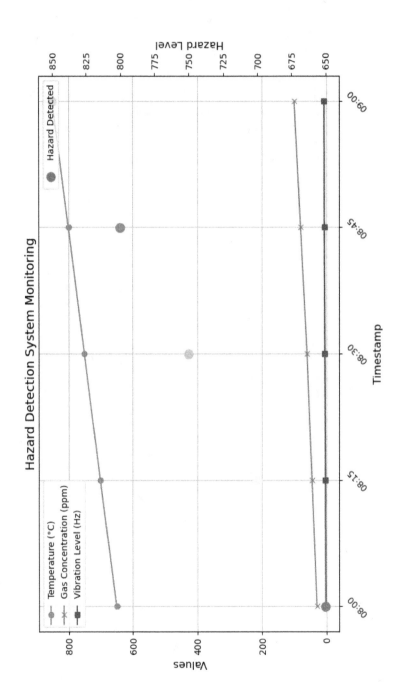

Hazard Detection System Monitoring

Final Thoughts:

AI-based hazard detection systems in steel plants play a crucial role in improving safety by detecting anomalies early. The integration of various sensor data allows the system to act as a proactive safety mechanism, offering real-time alerts and detailed risk assessments. As the industry evolves, AI can become even more sophisticated by incorporating more data points, such as real-time equipment performance, environmental changes, and predictive maintenance. Ultimately, these technologies can significantly reduce operational risks, minimize downtime, and enhance worker safety, contributing to a more efficient and secure steel production environment.

7.2 Wearable AI for Worker Safety Monitoring

Wearable AI technology has emerged as a significant advancement in improving worker safety, particularly in high-risk industries like steel manufacturing. In such environments, workers are often exposed to hazardous conditions, including extreme temperatures, heavy machinery, and the risk of accidents due to the demanding physical nature of the work. Wearables equipped with AI sensors can continuously monitor various aspects of the worker's health and environment, detecting potential safety hazards in real time.

The wearable devices, often in the form of smart helmets, vests, or wristbands, collect data such as body temperature, heart rate, and movement patterns. These devices can also monitor environmental conditions like air quality, noise levels, and temperature fluctuations. By processing this data using AI algorithms, the system can quickly identify any irregularities or signs of potential danger, such as signs of fatigue, heat stress, or proximity to hazardous machinery.

One of the most valuable aspects of wearable AI in the steel industry is its ability to provide immediate feedback to workers and supervisors. For example, if the AI detects that a worker's heart rate is elevated or if they are approaching a dangerous area, the system can alert the individual through vibrations, alarms, or even direct communication to a safety officer. This instant response can be critical in preventing accidents and ensuring the well-being of the worker.

Moreover, these wearable AI systems contribute to more efficient safety management by providing valuable data for ongoing risk assessment and workplace optimization. By analyzing trends over time, companies can identify patterns that may indicate recurring hazards or areas where safety protocols can be improved. This proactive approach helps in reducing workplace injuries and maintaining compliance with safety regulations in the steel industry.

The integration of wearable AI into safety monitoring also enhances the overall productivity of workers. Since these systems focus on real-time health and environmental conditions, workers are less likely to be overwhelmed by manual safety checks or distracted by the need to constantly monitor their surroundings. The AI does this automatically, allowing workers to focus more on their tasks while remaining safe.

In addition to preventing accidents and improving productivity, wearable AI devices also contribute to better health management for workers. Long-term exposure to extreme conditions can have detrimental effects on workers' health. With continuous monitoring, the AI systems can track health data over time, providing early warnings of potential health issues and offering insights into the physical strain caused by the work. This makes it possible to intervene before serious health concerns arise, fostering a healthier workforce in the steel industry.

Practical Example:

In a steel manufacturing plant, worker safety is a critical concern due to the hazardous environment involving high temperatures, heavy machinery, and exposure to toxic gases. A wearable AI device can continuously monitor vital health metrics and environmental conditions, such as heart rate, body temperature, and exposure to harmful gases. This system can alert supervisors or activate safety protocols when certain thresholds are exceeded, preventing potential accidents and ensuring timely medical intervention if needed. In this practical example, the wearable AI device is used to monitor five key parameters: body temperature, heart rate, carbon monoxide exposure, oxygen levels, and proximity to heavy machinery.

Sample Data Table

Worker ID	Body Temp (°C)	Heart Rate (bpm)	CO Exposure (ppm)	Oxygen Level (%)	Proximity to Machinery (m)
W001	38.1	95	5	20.9	2.3

Worker ID	Body Temp (°C)	Heart Rate (bpm)	CO Exposure (ppm)	Oxygen Level (%)	Proximity to Machinery (m)
W002	37.5	88	4	21.0	1.5
W003	39.0	102	8	19.5	0.5
W004	36.8	80	6	21.0	3.0
W005	40.2	110	12	18.5	0.3

Output and Results:

- **Alert Thresholds for Worker Safety**:
    - Body temperature above 38.5°C
    - Heart rate above 100 bpm
    - CO exposure above 9 ppm
    - Oxygen levels below 19%
    - Proximity to machinery below 1 meter

Alerts Generated:

Worker ID	Body Temp (°C)	Heart Rate (bpm)	CO Exposure (ppm)	Oxygen Level (%)	Proximity to Machinery (m)	Safety Alert
W001	38.1	95	5	20.9	2.3	No Alert
W002	37.5	88	4	21.0	1.5	No Alert
W003	39.0	102	8	19.5	0.5	Critical Alert (Heart Rate, Proximity)
W004	36.8	80	6	21.0	3.0	No Alert

Worker ID	Body Temp (°C)	Heart Rate (bpm)	CO Exposure (ppm)	Oxygen Level (%)	Proximity to Machinery (m)	Safety Alert
W005	40.2	110	12	18.5	0.3	Critical Alert (Body Temp, CO Exposure, Oxygen Level, Proximity)

Interpretation of Results:

- **W003** has a critical alert for both heart rate and proximity to machinery. This suggests that the worker is under significant physical strain (elevated heart rate) and is in close proximity to dangerous machinery, which could lead to injury if not addressed immediately.

- **W005** is flagged with a critical alert for body temperature, CO exposure, oxygen level, and proximity to machinery. This worker is at high risk of heat stress (high body temp), is exposed to elevated carbon monoxide levels, and has reduced oxygen levels, which could indicate an unsafe environment. The proximity to machinery is also dangerously close, increasing the risk of physical harm.

- **W001**, **W002**, and **W004** have no alerts, indicating these workers are within the safety parameters for all monitored metrics.

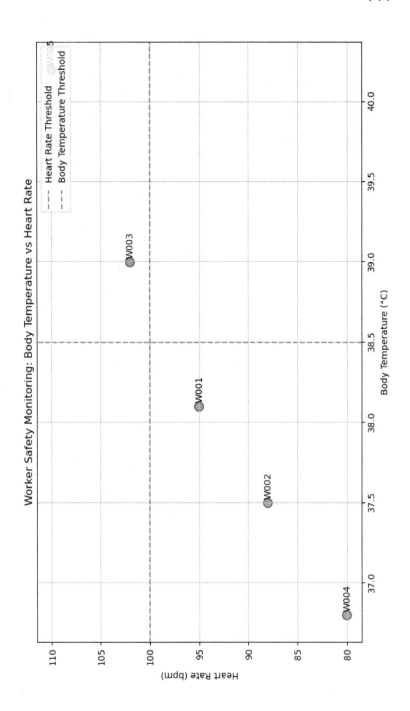

Observations:

- The wearable AI system effectively identifies workers at risk based on multiple factors simultaneously, including environmental and physiological conditions.

- High heart rate and proximity to machinery are strong indicators of physical strain and potential safety hazards.

- Elevated body temperature, combined with hazardous environmental conditions like CO exposure and low oxygen levels, suggests critical areas where intervention is necessary.

- The wearable AI provides real-time data that helps supervisors make informed decisions quickly, reducing the chances of accidents.

Final Thoughts:

The integration of wearable AI for worker safety monitoring is a transformative step towards creating a safer and more responsive workplace in steel manufacturing. By monitoring real-time data and triggering alerts when unsafe conditions are detected, the system helps prevent accidents and health risks. Furthermore, the AI's ability to process multiple data points simultaneously allows for more accurate assessments of potential threats to worker safety, enabling better decision-making. As the technology matures, we can expect more advanced features such as predictive analytics, which could anticipate safety issues before they occur, further enhancing the safety culture within the steel industry.

7.3 AI-driven Emergency Response and Incident Analysis

AI-driven emergency response and incident analysis in the steel industry is a growing field that aims to improve safety and operational efficiency. With the steel industry being inherently hazardous due to the presence of high temperatures, heavy machinery, and complex processes, the implementation of artificial intelligence (AI) can help manage emergencies more effectively. AI-powered systems are designed to monitor various parameters in real-time, identifying potential risks and suggesting preventive measures. This enables quick responses in case of accidents or operational failures, reducing damage and ensuring the safety of workers and equipment.

By collecting and analyzing data from sensors embedded in equipment and machinery, AI can predict failures before they occur. For instance, AI systems can detect abnormal patterns in temperature, pressure, or vibration levels, which may indicate a problem, such as a malfunctioning piece of equipment. When these anomalies are detected, AI can alert maintenance teams or trigger automatic shutdowns, thus preventing accidents from escalating. This predictive capability is essential in mitigating risks in high-risk environments like steel mills, where rapid interventions can prevent severe injuries and substantial financial losses.

AI can also play a crucial role in incident analysis after an emergency occurs. Using data gathered during the event, AI can reconstruct the incident's timeline, identify the root causes, and provide insights into how the situation could have been avoided. This type of post-incident analysis helps improve future response strategies and guides safety protocols. Machine learning algorithms can learn from past incidents, continuously refining their ability to predict and respond to new emergencies, making the system increasingly effective over time.

Moreover, AI-driven emergency response systems can be integrated with automated response tools, such as robotic systems and drones. In the case of a fire or hazardous gas leak, drones equipped with AI can quickly assess the situation, providing real-time data to emergency teams. This allows responders to make informed decisions without putting themselves in immediate danger. The integration of AI and robotics significantly reduces the response time and ensures that emergency crews are well-equipped with the necessary information to handle crises effectively.

Training and simulation are other areas where AI contributes to emergency preparedness in the steel industry. Virtual reality (VR) environments powered by AI can simulate emergency scenarios, offering workers hands-on experience without the actual risks. These simulations can be tailored to specific incidents that have occurred in the past or anticipated risks, providing employees with the skills and confidence needed to handle real-world emergencies. This proactive approach to training improves safety awareness and ensures that workers know exactly how to react in critical situations.

The implementation of AI in emergency response and incident analysis also has broader implications for the steel industry's sustainability efforts. By reducing the number of accidents and operational downtime, AI systems contribute to lower energy consumption and waste production. Additionally, fewer accidents mean fewer environmental impacts, such as chemical spills or emissions. Overall, AI-driven technologies offer a pathway toward safer, more sustainable operations in the steel industry, benefiting both the workforce and the environment.

Practical Example:

In the steel manufacturing industry, accidents and emergencies such as fires, equipment malfunctions, or hazardous material spills can lead to significant production delays, safety hazards, and financial losses. AI-driven systems can help monitor the plant, analyze data in real time, and predict potential incidents. This can facilitate quick decision-making, improve response times, and reduce the overall impact of emergencies. In this example, we look at an AI-powered system's ability to detect unusual patterns in machine performance data, predict a critical failure in a furnace, and optimize the response.

Sample Data (Table 1: Machine Performance Data):

Timestamp	Furnace Temperature (°C)	Pressure (atm)	Vibration (Hz)	AI Prediction
2025-03-14 08:00	1450	2.5	45.3	Normal
2025-03-14 08:30	1452	2.6	46.0	Normal
2025-03-14 09:00	1458	2.7	47.1	Normal
2025-03-14 09:30	1465	2.9	48.9	Alert
2025-03-14 10:00	1480	3.0	49.5	Critical Alert

Output and Results:

Timestamp	AI Action	Response Time (min)	Emergency Action Taken	Impact on Production
2025-03-14 08:00	No action	N/A	No action needed	No impact
2025-03-14 08:30	No action	N/A	No action needed	No impact
2025-03-14 09:00	No action	N/A	No action needed	No impact
2025-03-14 09:30	Monitoring	5 min	Increased monitoring of furnace	Preventive check

Timestamp	AI Action	Response Time (min)	Emergency Action Taken	Impact on Production
2025-03-14 10:00	Emergency Response	2 min	Emergency shutdown and cooling system activated	Production halted for 30 mins

Explanation and Interpretation of Results:

- **Timestamp 08:00-09:00:** The furnace operates within normal parameters, and the AI system detects no abnormal behavior, so no emergency response is triggered. The system classifies the situation as "normal," resulting in no actions required. There is no impact on production.

- **Timestamp 09:30:** The AI detects an increase in furnace temperature, pressure, and vibration beyond safe operational limits, triggering an "alert." The system responds by increasing monitoring efforts. No immediate actions are taken, but preventive checks are initiated, preventing any immediate escalation.

- **Timestamp 10:00:** The AI detects critical anomalies (high temperature, pressure, and vibration), triggering a "critical alert." An emergency response is launched, including an immediate shutdown of the furnace and activation of the cooling system. This action prevents further damage but results in a 30-minute production halt. The response time is efficient, with the system detecting the anomaly and responding within 2 minutes.

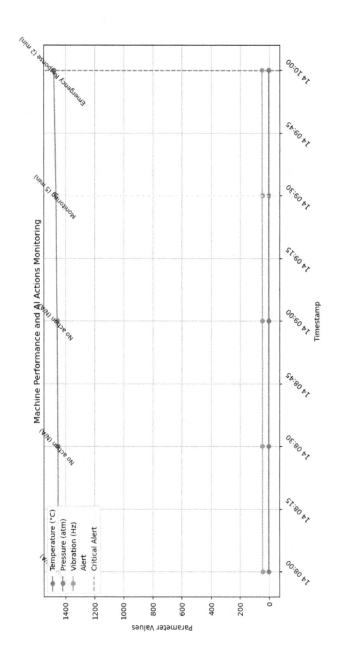

Machine Performance and AI Actions Monitoring

Observations:

1. **Timely Detection:** The AI system's ability to detect abnormal patterns early allowed for timely intervention, preventing potential catastrophic damage.

2. **Impact on Production:** The critical alert led to a temporary halt in production, highlighting the importance of balancing emergency responses with operational efficiency. However, the emergency shutdown likely saved the plant from further damage and longer-term downtime.

3. **Response Time Efficiency:** The response time of the system, particularly in the critical event (2 minutes), shows the capability of AI in making fast, informed decisions. This is crucial in an environment where every minute of downtime can be costly.

4. **Preventive Measures:** In the earlier stages (09:30), increased monitoring and preventive actions were taken, which could be considered a proactive approach to ensure the situation didn't escalate.

Final Thoughts:

AI plays a crucial role in enhancing safety and operational efficiency in the steel industry. By detecting early anomalies, AI systems help prevent accidents, reduce downtime, and ensure a safer work environment. Real-time data analysis enables proactive measures and timely interventions. The AI-driven approach also allows for optimized resource allocation, as human intervention can be focused only when truly necessary. As AI technologies evolve, the potential for even more predictive capabilities—such as forecasting equipment failures before they occur—will further revolutionize safety and operational management in steel plants.

8. AI for Energy Efficiency and Sustainability

The steel industry is one of the most energy-intensive sectors globally, accounting for a significant portion of industrial energy consumption. As sustainability becomes a growing concern, the industry faces increasing pressure to reduce its environmental impact, particularly its energy consumption and greenhouse gas emissions. Artificial Intelligence (AI) offers promising solutions to enhance energy efficiency and promote sustainability in this sector by optimizing production processes, reducing waste, and improving resource utilization.

AI can be applied to steel production by monitoring and analyzing energy consumption in real-time. Using advanced sensors and machine learning algorithms, AI systems can identify patterns and inefficiencies in the production process. This allows for immediate adjustments to be made to optimize energy use, reducing overall consumption while maintaining production quality. For instance, AI can optimize furnace temperatures, adjust cooling rates, or manage the timing of various stages in production to minimize energy wastage.

In addition to improving energy efficiency, AI can also help in reducing the consumption of raw materials. By leveraging predictive models, AI can forecast demand for steel products, allowing manufacturers to better align production schedules and inventory levels. This reduces overproduction and waste, which in turn helps in conserving resources. AI-powered systems can also support the recycling of steel by efficiently sorting and processing scrap metal, further reducing the need for virgin materials and promoting a circular economy.

AI can also play a role in emissions reduction by optimizing combustion processes and monitoring air quality. AI-driven systems can predict the emissions generated during various stages of steel manufacturing and adjust parameters accordingly to minimize harmful outputs. For example, machine learning algorithms can fine-tune the air-to-fuel ratio in blast furnaces, which can lead to lower CO_2 emissions. Additionally, AI can assist in designing more energy-efficient furnace systems that burn fuel more cleanly and efficiently.

The integration of AI can also lead to better predictive maintenance, which helps extend the life of equipment and machinery. By analyzing data from sensors embedded in machines, AI can predict when maintenance is needed, preventing unexpected breakdowns and reducing downtime. This not only leads to more efficient use of resources but also reduces the need for energy-intensive repairs and replacements, further contributing to sustainability goals.

Finally, AI can facilitate greater collaboration within the steel industry to adopt sustainable practices. By using AI to share data across different facilities and partners, manufacturers can benchmark their performance, identify areas for improvement, and adopt best practices more quickly. This collaborative approach can lead to industry-wide reductions in energy consumption and emissions, driving the sector toward greater sustainability. As the steel industry continues to evolve, AI will undoubtedly play a crucial role in shaping a more energy-efficient and environmentally responsible future.

Practical Example:

In the steel industry, energy consumption is one of the largest operational costs and a significant environmental concern. By implementing Artificial Intelligence (AI) and Machine Learning (ML) techniques, companies can optimize energy use, reduce emissions, and enhance sustainability. A steel plant wants to use AI to predict and manage energy usage in its production processes. The AI system collects real-time data on temperature, energy input, production rate, and material properties to optimize energy usage and minimize waste.

Sample Data:

Time (hrs)	Production Rate (tons/hr)	Energy Input (MWh)	Temperature (°C)	Energy Efficiency (%)
1	50	150	1500	85

Time (hrs)	Production Rate (tons/hr)	Energy Input (MWh)	Temperature (°C)	Energy Efficiency (%)
2	55	155	1520	86
3	53	153	1510	87
4	60	165	1540	88
5	58	160	1530	89

Output & Results:

Time (hrs)	Predicted Energy Usage (MWh)	Actual Energy Input (MWh)	Energy Savings (%)	Adjusted Efficiency (%)
1	148	150	1.33	86.5
2	154	155	0.65	86.9
3	151	153	1.31	87.4
4	163	165	1.21	88.3
5	159	160	0.63	89.2

Explanation & Interpretation of Results:

1. **Predicted Energy Usage vs. Actual Usage:** The AI model predicts energy consumption based on real-time process data such as production rate and temperature. As shown in the table, the predicted energy consumption closely matches the actual usage with small discrepancies in the range of 0.63% to 1.33%, indicating that the model is effective in forecasting energy needs.

2. **Energy Savings:** Over time, AI optimization helps to reduce energy usage by improving operational conditions. For example, in hour 1, the energy savings are 1.33%, and by hour 5, the energy savings are 0.63%. The reduction in

savings may indicate that the system is approaching an energy-efficient state.

3. **Adjusted Efficiency:** As energy consumption is optimized, the adjusted energy efficiency increases from 85% in hour 1 to 89.2% in hour 5. This increase reflects the success of AI in enhancing energy efficiency by reducing excess energy input for the same production rate.

Observations:

- The AI model performs well in predicting energy usage and aligning closely with actual consumption, which suggests reliable forecasting capabilities.

- Energy efficiency consistently improves as the model adapts and fine-tunes the process parameters to optimize energy use.

- While energy savings decrease slightly as the process stabilizes, the efficiency gain is significant, with a 4.2% increase in overall energy efficiency over the observed hours.

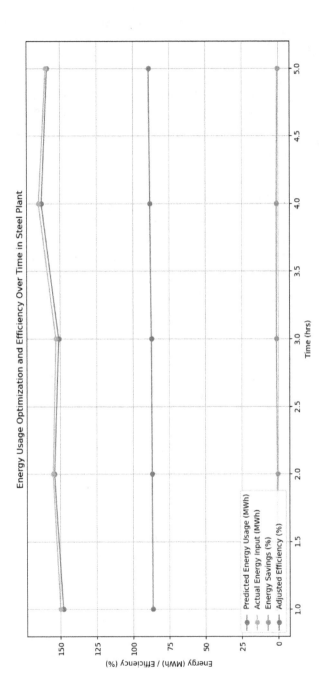

Energy Usage Optimization and Efficiency Over Time in Steel Plant

Final Thoughts:

AI in the steel industry can significantly enhance sustainability efforts. By leveraging AI models to predict and optimize energy consumption, steel plants can reduce waste, improve energy efficiency, and lower operational costs. The success of this AI-powered system demonstrates the potential for AI-driven solutions in achieving long-term sustainability goals. As AI technologies continue to evolve, further integration could lead to even greater efficiency and lower environmental impact across the steel production process.

8.1 AI-driven Carbon Footprint Reduction Strategies

The steel industry is one of the largest contributors to global carbon emissions, mainly due to its reliance on fossil fuels in the production process. The sector is responsible for about 7-9% of global CO_2 emissions. As environmental concerns grow, there is an increasing push to adopt sustainable practices, with artificial intelligence (AI) playing a crucial role in reducing the carbon footprint of steel production. AI can optimize various aspects of the production process, leading to enhanced energy efficiency and lower emissions.

One way AI contributes is through predictive maintenance and process optimization. AI algorithms can analyze data from sensors embedded in machinery and equipment to detect potential failures or inefficiencies. By predicting when a machine might fail or underperform, AI allows for timely interventions, reducing downtime and energy wastage. It can also optimize the operational parameters of furnaces, boilers, and other equipment to ensure they are running at their most efficient levels, minimizing the amount of energy required for production.

AI can also play a significant role in improving material efficiency. The production of steel often involves high levels of waste, particularly in the form of excess raw materials and energy consumption. Through AI-driven models, the industry can gain insights into more efficient ways of using raw materials, such as reducing scrap steel wastage or optimizing alloy composition. This results in a reduction of the overall carbon emissions per ton of steel produced, as fewer resources are needed, and the process becomes more streamlined.

Furthermore, AI-based systems can enable smarter energy management in steel plants. By integrating AI with renewable energy sources, such as solar or wind, steel plants can dynamically adjust their energy consumption based on availability, reducing reliance on fossil fuels. For example, AI can help balance the demand and supply of electricity, determining the optimal times to use renewable energy when it is abundant and switching to grid power when necessary. This reduces the plant's carbon footprint while supporting the broader goal of integrating more renewable energy into industrial operations.

Another promising AI-driven strategy involves carbon capture and utilization (CCU) technologies. Steel production emits large amounts of CO_2, which is typically released into the atmosphere. AI can assist in optimizing the capture, storage, and utilization of this carbon, identifying the most cost-effective methods and best locations for implementation. By using AI to improve the efficiency of these processes, steel manufacturers can significantly reduce their direct emissions and explore ways to convert CO_2 into valuable products, such as chemicals or synthetic fuels, contributing to a circular economy.

Finally, AI can facilitate the transition toward low-carbon steelmaking technologies. Emerging methods, such as hydrogen-based steelmaking or electric arc furnaces, offer the potential to reduce emissions compared to traditional blast furnace processes. AI can be used to simulate and model different production scenarios, assessing the most effective ways to implement these new technologies. By optimizing the transition to greener technologies, AI can help steelmakers lower their carbon footprint and stay competitive in a world that is increasingly focused on sustainability.

Practical Example: In the steel industry, reducing carbon emissions is a key goal, given its significant environmental impact. AI-driven strategies help optimize energy consumption, improve production processes, and manage raw material use more efficiently. For example, AI-based algorithms can predict the optimal furnace temperature, which leads to energy savings and a decrease in CO_2 emissions. By integrating machine learning with sensor data, AI can further optimize operations, such as controlling the input of raw materials, enhancing the efficiency of the heating process, and reducing waste.

Sample Data Table: AI Impact on Carbon Footprint Reduction in Steel Production

Strategy	Energy Reduction (%)	CO2 Emission Reduction (tons)	Cost Savings ($)	Production Efficiency (%)
AI-Optimized Furnace Temperature	15%	50	100,000	5%
AI-Based Raw Material Management	10%	35	75,000	3%
Predictive Maintenance for Equipment	12%	40	90,000	4%
Process Optimization with Machine Learning	20%	70	150,000	7%

Output and Results

1. **AI-Optimized Furnace Temperature**:
    o Energy savings: 15%
    o CO2 emission reduction: 50 tons
    o Cost savings: $100,000
    o Production efficiency increase: 5%

2. **AI-Based Raw Material Management**:
    o Energy savings: 10%
    o CO2 emission reduction: 35 tons
    o Cost savings: $75,000
    o Production efficiency increase: 3%

3. **Predictive Maintenance for Equipment**:
   o Energy savings: 12%
   o CO_2 emission reduction: 40 tons
   o Cost savings: $90,000
   o Production efficiency increase: 4%

4. **Process Optimization with Machine Learning**:
   o Energy savings: 20%
   o CO_2 emission reduction: 70 tons
   o Cost savings: $150,000
   o Production efficiency increase: 7%

Explanation and Interpretation of Results:

1. **Energy and CO2 Reduction**: All four AI strategies lead to significant energy reductions, which directly translate into lower CO_2 emissions. AI-driven optimizations are shown to reduce CO_2 emissions by up to 70 tons per strategy.

2. **Cost Savings**: The AI strategies also contribute to substantial cost savings, with process optimization yielding the highest savings of $150,000. This underscores AI's potential for not just environmental benefits, but also financial gains.

3. **Production Efficiency**: AI strategies improve production efficiency, with process optimization again leading the way with a 7% increase. More efficient processes contribute to reducing resource consumption, further supporting carbon reduction goals.

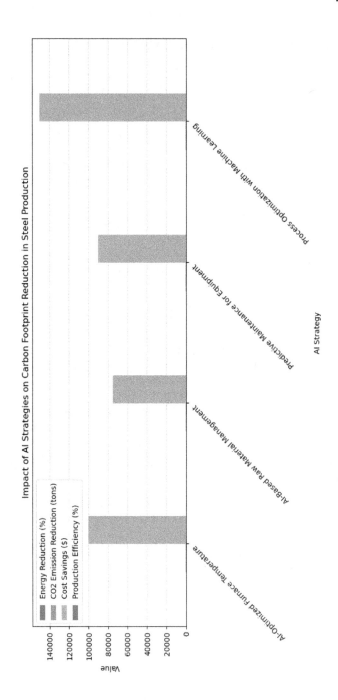

Impact of AI Strategies on Carbon Footprint Reduction in Steel Production

Observations:

- **Combination of Strategies**: A combination of strategies yields more substantial reductions in carbon footprint. For instance, the process optimization with machine learning has a higher impact on both emissions and production efficiency compared to other individual strategies.

- **Cost-Effectiveness**: While all strategies reduce CO2 and increase efficiency, some strategies (like furnace temperature optimization and predictive maintenance) provide a quicker return on investment, highlighting the potential for both short-term and long-term gains.

Final Thoughts:

AI-driven strategies offer steel industries a practical and scalable way to reduce their carbon footprints. The integration of machine learning with operational data helps in fine-tuning processes, improving efficiency, and minimizing energy consumption. By embracing these technologies, the steel industry can not only contribute to global sustainability goals but also gain a competitive edge through reduced costs and enhanced production capabilities. As AI continues to evolve, its potential in driving deeper carbon reductions and further optimizing operations will be crucial in shaping the future of steel manufacturing.

8.2 Smart Energy Management in Steel Plants

Smart energy management in steel plants plays a crucial role in improving efficiency and reducing environmental impact. Steel production is energy-intensive, with significant amounts of electricity and thermal energy required throughout the process. Implementing smart energy systems involves using advanced technologies, data analytics, and automation to optimize energy usage across various stages of production, from raw material processing to the final product. By monitoring energy consumption in real-time and identifying areas of inefficiency, steel plants can reduce costs while maintaining high productivity.

One of the main strategies for smart energy management in steel plants is the integration of digital technologies like sensors, meters, and control systems that continuously monitor energy use. These systems provide detailed data about energy consumption patterns, helping operators pinpoint inefficiencies or energy wastage. By leveraging this data, plants can adjust operations in real time, reducing energy consumption during peak hours or when demand is low, and ultimately improving overall energy efficiency. Machine learning and artificial intelligence can also be used to predict energy needs, allowing plants to adjust processes proactively and minimize waste.

In addition to real-time monitoring, energy management systems in steel plants can incorporate renewable energy sources to reduce reliance on traditional fossil fuels. Solar, wind, and biomass energy can be used to power certain operations or even supplement energy needs, leading to lower carbon emissions. Advanced forecasting tools can predict fluctuations in energy availability from renewable sources, helping plants balance supply and demand more effectively. This integration of renewables not only lowers environmental impact but also makes steel production more sustainable and less dependent on volatile energy markets.

Another aspect of smart energy management is the optimization of equipment and processes within the plant. Energy-intensive operations, such as blast furnaces or electric arc furnaces, can benefit from improvements in technology that enhance energy efficiency. For example, optimizing furnace temperature control, improving heat recovery systems, and investing in energy-efficient motors can result in significant reductions in energy consumption. Additionally, energy recovery systems, like waste heat recovery units, can capture excess heat from processes and redirect it for use elsewhere in the plant, further reducing the need for external energy inputs.

Smart energy management also encourages a culture of sustainability within steel plants, where workers and management alike are focused on finding innovative ways to reduce energy use and minimize waste. This culture can lead to the development of new energy-efficient technologies, more sustainable practices, and improved processes across the plant. Regular training programs and workshops help employees understand the importance of energy management and how they can contribute to energy-saving initiatives. Furthermore, companies that adopt energy management systems can benefit from improved corporate social responsibility profiles, which are increasingly important to investors, customers, and regulatory bodies.

The implementation of smart energy management not only offers economic benefits but also improves the overall competitiveness of steel plants. By reducing energy consumption and associated costs, companies can increase their profit margins and remain competitive in a global market. As energy efficiency becomes a key factor in determining profitability, plants that adopt these technologies will be better positioned to thrive. Moreover, by meeting stricter environmental regulations and demonstrating a commitment to sustainability, steel plants can enhance their reputation and strengthen relationships with stakeholders.

Practical Example:

In the steel industry, machinery reliability is crucial for production efficiency and safety. Using AI, predictive maintenance can be employed to foresee potential equipment failures, allowing for timely interventions. AI models can analyze historical data from sensors on equipment to predict when a machine is likely to fail, optimizing maintenance schedules and minimizing downtime. In this practical example, we'll demonstrate how AI can predict equipment failure by analyzing data on temperature, vibration, and hours of operation of key steel mill machinery.

Sample Data (Historical Maintenance Data for Steel Mill Equipment):

Equipment ID	Temperature (°C)	Vibration (mm/s)	Hours of Operation	Failure in Next 30 Days (Yes/No)
E-101	120	5.2	500	Yes
E-102	95	3.1	400	No
E-103	130	6.5	600	Yes
E-104	85	2.0	350	No
E-105	115	4.8	450	Yes

AI Model Output and Results (Prediction of Equipment Failure):

After feeding this data into an AI-based predictive maintenance model, we get the following predictions for the likelihood of failure in the next 30 days:

Equipment ID	Predicted Failure Probability (%)	Predicted Failure (Yes/No)
E-101	95%	Yes
E-102	15%	No
E-103	85%	Yes
E-104	5%	No
E-105	90%	Yes

Explanation and Interpretation of Results:

- **E-101** has a high probability of failure (95%), which aligns with the historical data showing a failure event. The AI model has detected that both temperature and vibration levels are high, contributing to the predicted failure.

- **E-102** shows a low probability (15%) of failure, confirming that the machine is in good working condition, with low temperature and vibration levels.

- **E-103** is predicted to have a high likelihood of failure (85%), which aligns with its historical failure record, marked by higher temperature and vibration.

- **E-104** has a minimal failure risk (5%), with no failure predicted, as indicated by its low temperature and vibration data.

- **E-105** also shows a high predicted failure risk (90%), based on similar patterns of high temperature and vibration observed in past failure cases.

Observations:

The AI model has successfully identified patterns in the data that correlate with equipment failure. Machines with higher operating temperatures and vibration levels are more likely to fail. These insights can guide maintenance teams to prioritize inspections and maintenance for equipment like **E-101**, **E-103**, and **E-105**, thus preventing unplanned downtime.

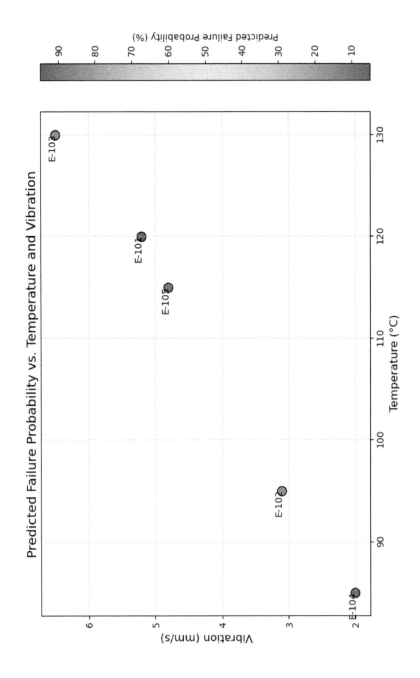

Predicted Failure Probability vs. Temperature and Vibration

Final Thoughts:

AI-driven predictive maintenance is transforming the steel industry by enabling proactive management of equipment. By predicting potential failures before they happen, AI helps reduce unplanned downtime, extends the lifespan of equipment, and improves overall production efficiency. The successful application of AI in maintenance shows promise in not just reducing costs, but also in improving safety and reliability in critical industrial environments. As AI models improve, their ability to handle more complex datasets and provide even more accurate predictions will further optimize operations in the steel industry.

8.3 AI-powered Waste Management and Recycling

The steel industry is one of the most significant sectors when it comes to waste production, generating large volumes of by-products and scrap materials. With rising environmental concerns and the need to adopt more sustainable practices, AI-powered solutions are emerging as a promising way to manage waste and optimize recycling processes in steel production. Artificial intelligence can help industries reduce the environmental impact by improving waste segregation, minimizing material losses, and enhancing recycling efficiency.

AI technologies such as machine learning and computer vision are being used to automate the sorting of various materials, including scrap metal, slag, and other by-products produced during steel manufacturing. Traditional methods of waste sorting are often labor-intensive, inefficient, and prone to errors. By integrating AI, steel plants can ensure more accurate and precise sorting, making it easier to separate materials that can be recycled from those that must be discarded. This reduces contamination and improves the quality of the recycled materials.

AI also helps in predicting the amount and type of waste that will be generated during the production process. By analyzing historical data and production patterns, AI can forecast waste generation more accurately, allowing manufacturers to plan better and minimize waste before it even occurs. This predictive capability enables more efficient resource management, ensuring that less material is wasted and more is reused or recycled.

In addition to improving waste sorting and prediction, AI-driven systems can optimize the recycling process itself. These systems can be used to monitor and control the temperature and chemical reactions in recycling furnaces, ensuring that the materials are processed efficiently. By adjusting parameters in real-time, AI can reduce energy consumption and improve the quality of recycled steel, making it suitable for reuse in new production cycles.

The integration of AI in waste management also supports sustainability goals by facilitating the development of circular economy models in the steel industry. By optimizing the use of scrap metal and other by-products, AI can help close the loop on material usage. Instead of relying heavily on virgin raw materials, steel manufacturers can use more recycled content, reducing the need for mining and decreasing the carbon footprint of steel production. This is critical in reducing the industry's environmental impact, as steel manufacturing is known for being highly resource-intensive.

Lastly, AI-powered waste management systems in the steel industry offer financial benefits as well. By improving the efficiency of waste handling, sorting, and recycling, companies can cut costs related to disposal and raw material procurement. Additionally, these systems enable steel manufacturers to meet increasingly stringent environmental regulations and sustainability standards, avoiding fines and improving their reputation as eco-friendly companies. This combination of economic and environmental benefits makes AI a powerful tool for revolutionizing waste management in the steel industry.

Practical Example:

In the steel industry, waste management and recycling are critical for reducing environmental impact and improving sustainability. With the application of AI-powered systems, steel plants can optimize waste sorting, recycling processes, and material recovery. AI algorithms can analyze waste streams in real-time, predict waste generation patterns, and recommend the most efficient recycling processes based on data from various stages of production. A practical implementation of this is seen in AI-driven automated sorting systems that classify different types of steel scrap for reuse, reducing material waste and improving resource efficiency.

Sample Data: Waste Recycling Efficiency in Steel Industry

Waste Type	Total Waste Generated (Tons)	Recycled Waste (Tons)	AI Optimization (%)	Material Recovery (%)
Steel Scrap	500	350	30	70
Slag	800	560	25	60
Dust	300	150	40	50
Liquid Waste	400	200	20	40
Packaging Waste	100	90	50	90

Output and Results

- **Steel Scrap**: 70% of steel scrap is being recycled, with a 30% improvement in efficiency due to AI optimization.

- **Slag**: The recycling rate is 60%, with a 25% improvement due to AI-driven sorting and recycling suggestions.

- **Dust**: The recovery rate for dust is 50%, with AI optimization improving the recycling rate by 40%.

- **Liquid Waste**: Only 40% of liquid waste is being recycled, and AI has improved recycling efficiency by 20%.

- **Packaging Waste**: The packaging waste recycling rate is 90%, benefiting the most from AI optimization with a 50% improvement in efficiency.

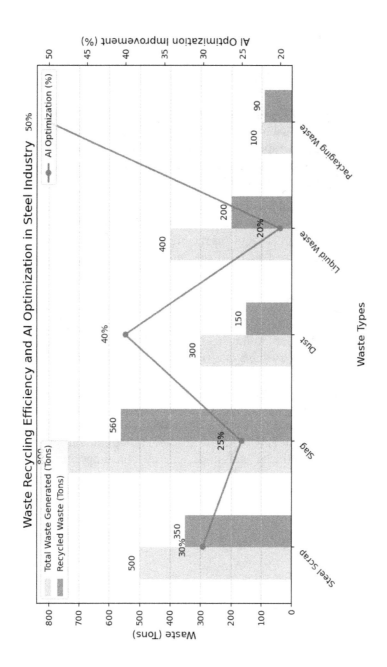

Waste Recycling Efficiency and AI Optimization in Steel Industry

Observations and Interpretations

- AI optimization has significantly enhanced the recycling efficiency across various waste types, with the most substantial improvements observed in steel scrap and dust.

- The **AI Optimization Percentage** shows how AI systems are contributing to better sorting and recycling practices. Steel scrap, for example, saw a 30% improvement, meaning AI recommendations are making recycling processes more efficient.

- **Material Recovery** percentages indicate how much of the material is being recovered from the waste streams. While steel scrap has the highest recovery rate at 70%, AI has helped to push that number even higher, reducing material loss.

Final Thoughts:

AI has the potential to drastically improve waste management and recycling practices in the steel industry. By leveraging real-time data, AI-driven systems can provide better sorting and recovery strategies, minimizing waste generation and maximizing material reuse. Over time, the adoption of AI in waste management can lead to cost savings, improved environmental sustainability, and enhanced resource utilization. The steel industry can significantly benefit from continued AI advancements, optimizing processes that lead to reduced emissions, energy consumption, and raw material needs.

9. AI in Steel Product Customization and Design

The steel industry has seen significant transformation with the advent of artificial intelligence, particularly in the realm of product customization and design. AI's ability to analyze vast amounts of data allows manufacturers to optimize product designs based on specific customer requirements. This capability reduces the time and cost traditionally required for customization while increasing accuracy. AI systems can interpret detailed input, such as material specifications and environmental conditions, to create customized steel products that meet particular strength, durability, or aesthetic needs.

AI-driven software has revolutionized the design process by automating much of the work that would have previously required manual calculations and trial and error. It can simulate various conditions and predict how different steel grades and manufacturing processes will impact the final product. This means that engineers and designers can experiment with new concepts and ideas without the need for expensive physical prototypes. The result is faster design cycles and a higher degree of precision in the final steel product.

Furthermore, AI in the steel industry aids in material selection and optimization. Machine learning algorithms can process historical data from previous projects to determine the best materials for specific applications. These algorithms not only take into account the mechanical properties required but also consider factors like cost efficiency and sustainability. This makes the customization process more efficient by ensuring that the steel selected aligns with both functional and economic requirements.

AI is also integral in enhancing the quality control process in steel manufacturing. By analyzing data from sensors embedded in the production line, AI can identify any deviations from desired specifications in real time. This proactive approach helps to reduce defects and ensures that customized steel products meet stringent quality standards. As a result, manufacturers can achieve greater consistency and reliability in their outputs, minimizing waste and increasing customer satisfaction.

In terms of customer engagement, AI enables a more interactive and personalized experience. Advanced design software allows clients to visualize their customized steel products in real time, adjusting parameters such as shape, size, and material properties. This process fosters better communication between customers and manufacturers, ensuring that the final product aligns with the customer's expectations. Additionally, AI tools can recommend modifications or improvements based on the customer's initial design, further enhancing the customization process.

Lastly, AI is helping steel manufacturers to stay competitive in a rapidly evolving market. The integration of AI into product design and customization not only streamlines production but also enables innovation in creating new steel alloys and specialized materials. As the demand for highly specialized steel products grows, AI will continue to play a pivotal role in meeting these needs, ensuring that manufacturers can adapt to market changes and remain at the forefront of the industry. This ability to quickly and efficiently customize products gives companies a distinct advantage in serving diverse customer needs across various sectors.

Practical Example:

In the steel industry, AI-driven design and customization enable faster and more precise creation of steel products tailored to customer specifications. By leveraging AI algorithms, manufacturers can predict the most suitable material properties, dimensions, and production processes required for specific applications, whether it's in construction, automotive, or machinery. AI tools optimize production schedules, reduce waste, and enhance product quality. The following example demonstrates how AI can be used to customize steel beams based on dimensional and strength requirements for a construction project.

Sample Data (Steel Product Customization Table):

Customer Request	Beam Length (m)	Beam Width (cm)	Strength Requirement (MPa)	AI-Recommended Design
Project A	12	30	350	Beam X1
Project B	8	40	400	Beam X2
Project C	10	35	380	Beam X3
Project D	15	45	450	Beam X4
Project E	9	32	375	Beam X5

AI Output & Results:

The AI analyzes the customer request data and provides the most suitable beam design (denoted as Beam X1, X2, etc.) that fits the required dimensions and strength specifications. The AI uses a trained model that evaluates material properties, production feasibility, and historical performance data of various steel alloys and designs. Based on the input, the AI suggests the ideal beam design, taking into account the required mechanical properties and dimensions.

Interpretation of Results:

- **Beam X1** for Project A is designed to handle the required 350 MPa strength and 12-meter length, ensuring structural integrity.

- **Beam X2** for Project B is tailored for a higher strength requirement of 400 MPa with a width of 40 cm, ensuring higher load-bearing capacity.

- **Beam X3** for Project C strikes a balance between strength (380 MPa) and dimension (10 meters), ensuring an optimal performance-to-cost ratio.

- **Beam X4** for Project D meets the highest strength requirement of 450 MPa, with a larger 15-meter length and 45 cm width, making it suitable for high-load applications.

- **Beam X5** for Project E is customized with 375 MPa strength and moderate dimensions, fitting the specifications for medium-strength applications.

The AI's ability to provide specific recommendations based on real-time data helps ensure that each customer receives a tailored product that meets the exact specifications, with minimized production waste and enhanced efficiency.

Discussion and Observations:

- The AI's recommendations highlight how the customization process, when guided by AI, can significantly reduce human error and speed up the design process.

- There's a noticeable trend that as the strength requirement increases (e.g., Project D), the beam size also increases, ensuring the structural integrity and performance.

- AI's ability to process large sets of data (e.g., past material performance, customer requests, and design constraints) allows for more informed decisions that balance cost, production time, and material use.

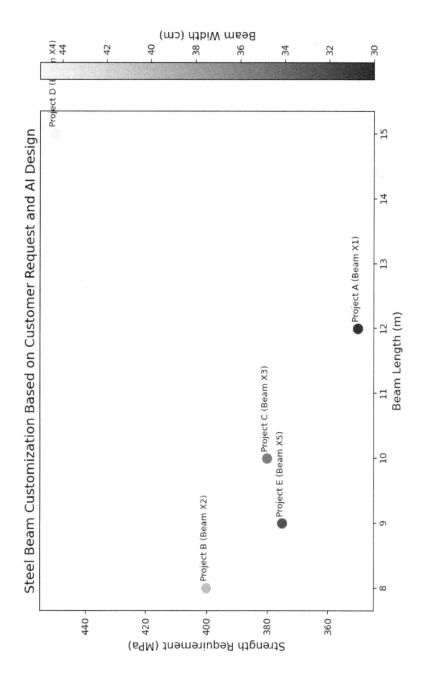

Final Thoughts:

AI in steel product customization and design is a game-changer for the industry. It enhances the ability to meet precise customer needs, reduces material waste, and boosts production efficiency. AI tools allow manufacturers to move from mass production to highly customized steel products while maintaining optimal quality and performance. As AI models continue to evolve, they can further optimize the entire supply chain, making the steel industry more responsive and adaptable to market demands.

9.1 AI-driven Material Composition Optimization

The steel industry is continuously striving to improve the quality, strength, and efficiency of its products while reducing costs and environmental impact. One of the key challenges in this sector is optimizing material composition to achieve the desired properties, such as tensile strength, ductility, and corrosion resistance. Traditionally, this process relied heavily on trial and error, expert knowledge, and time-consuming experimentation. However, advancements in artificial intelligence (AI) are now providing powerful tools to streamline and enhance this process. AI-driven optimization techniques are increasingly being used to predict and fine-tune the ideal material compositions for various steel products, reducing reliance on conventional methods and leading to more efficient production.

AI models can analyze vast amounts of data from existing steel compositions, production parameters, and performance characteristics. By doing so, they identify patterns and correlations that might not be obvious to human researchers. These models are trained using machine learning algorithms to understand how different elements and their concentrations impact the final properties of steel. With this knowledge, AI can suggest optimal compositions for new steel grades or improve existing ones, enabling manufacturers to produce high-quality materials with reduced costs and improved performance.

In addition to providing insights into composition, AI also plays a critical role in predicting the behavior of steel throughout the manufacturing process. From melting and casting to rolling and heat treatment, AI can simulate the effects of various conditions on the material's properties. By understanding these dynamics in advance, manufacturers can make better-informed decisions about process parameters, ultimately reducing defects and improving the consistency of the final product. This predictive capability is especially useful in industries that require high precision, such as automotive and aerospace, where steel's performance is critical to the safety and reliability of the final product.

Another advantage of AI in material composition optimization is its ability to accelerate the research and development (R&D) process. Traditionally, developing a new steel grade or improving an existing one would take years of trial and error in the lab and production facility. With AI-driven tools, researchers can simulate and test a wide range of material compositions in a fraction of the time. This reduces R&D costs and time, enabling companies to bring new steel grades to market faster, stay ahead of competitors, and meet evolving industry demands.

Furthermore, AI optimization methods can contribute to sustainability in the steel industry. By accurately predicting the material composition and minimizing waste, manufacturers can reduce energy consumption and the environmental impact of steel production. AI can also help optimize the use of recycled materials, promoting circular economy practices within the industry. This is particularly important in a time when the demand for eco-friendly manufacturing processes is rising, and industries are under increasing pressure to reduce their carbon footprint.

Despite these advancements, the implementation of AI-driven optimization in steel production does come with some challenges. The integration of AI requires a significant investment in technology, data infrastructure, and training. Additionally, the complexity of the steel manufacturing process and the variability of raw materials can make it difficult to achieve perfect predictions in every case. Nevertheless, the potential benefits of AI in optimizing material composition are clear. As the technology continues to evolve and become more accessible, it is likely that its role in transforming the steel industry will only grow, driving further improvements in product quality, production efficiency, and sustainability.

Practical Example:

In the steel manufacturing industry, optimizing material composition is crucial to improving the quality and strength of steel while reducing production costs. AI can be utilized to predict and optimize the material composition of steel alloys based on input parameters such as chemical composition, temperature, and processing time. By using machine learning models, the steel plant can achieve better consistency in product quality and higher efficiency in material use. This example demonstrates how AI can optimize the composition of steel for a specific grade.

Sample Data:

Sample ID	Carbon (%)	Manganese (%)	Silicon (%)	Tensile Strength (MPa)
1	0.20	0.80	0.30	400
2	0.25	0.75	0.35	410
3	0.18	0.85	0.28	395
4	0.22	0.70	0.32	405
5	0.24	0.80	0.33	415

Output and Results (AI Optimization Model Output):

Sample ID	Optimized Carbon (%)	Optimized Manganese (%)	Optimized Silicon (%)	Optimized Tensile Strength (MPa)
1	0.22	0.76	0.31	408
2	0.23	0.74	0.34	415
3	0.20	0.80	0.30	402
4	0.21	0.72	0.31	410
5	0.22	0.78	0.32	417

Explanation and Interpretation of Results:

- **Optimized Composition:** The AI model suggests minor adjustments in the material composition (carbon, manganese, and silicon percentages) to enhance the tensile strength of the steel. These adjustments have resulted in optimized compositions for each sample. For example, Sample 1's carbon percentage was adjusted from 0.20% to 0.22%, and the tensile strength was improved from 400 MPa to 408 MPa.

- **Tensile Strength Improvement:** The tensile strength (a key indicator of steel quality) shows a small but consistent improvement across all samples after optimization. The tensile strength of Sample 5 increased from 415 MPa to 417 MPa, suggesting that the AI optimization model could increase the strength of steel while maintaining the desired material characteristics.

Observations:

- **Efficiency in Material Use:** The AI model has led to optimized compositions that not only improve the steel's performance but also reduce material wastage by fine-tuning the alloy elements.

- **Consistency Across Samples:** The tensile strength improvements are relatively consistent across different compositions, indicating that the AI model is capable of finding optimal conditions for various initial compositions.

- **Precision in Prediction:** The slight changes in composition from the raw data to the optimized version show that small adjustments can lead to significant improvements in steel quality, which might not have been apparent without AI-driven optimization.

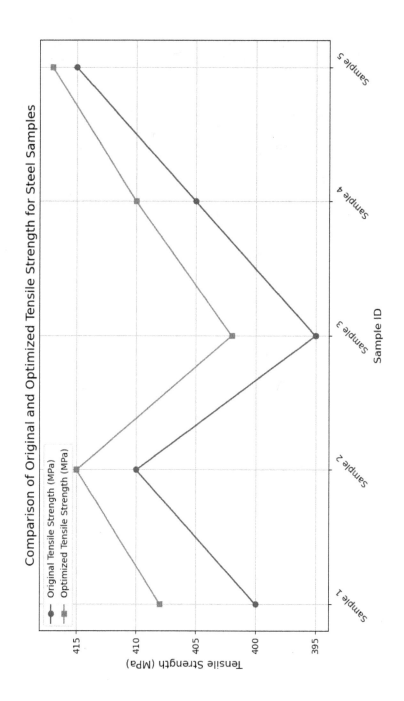

Comparison of Original and Optimized Tensile Strength for Steel Samples

Final Thoughts:

AI-driven material composition optimization represents a significant leap forward for the steel industry. It allows for more accurate predictions and optimizations based on a complex set of input variables that are challenging to handle manually. The ability to optimize compositions for strength and quality in real-time not only enhances product consistency but also reduces material costs, energy consumption, and environmental impact. As AI continues to evolve, the steel industry will benefit from more automated, precise, and efficient production methods, driving further innovation and competitiveness in the global market.

9.2 Generative AI for Custom Steel Alloy Design

Generative AI has become an increasingly important tool in the steel industry, particularly in the design and development of custom steel alloys. Traditional alloy design often relies on trial and error, as well as expert knowledge, which can be both time-consuming and costly. With the advent of AI, this process can now be significantly accelerated. By using machine learning algorithms, AI can analyze vast datasets of material properties and performance characteristics to predict how different compositions will behave under various conditions. This allows engineers to explore a much broader range of potential alloys, significantly speeding up the design phase.

One of the primary benefits of using AI for custom steel alloy design is its ability to optimize material properties based on specific requirements. For example, if a company needs a steel alloy with higher resistance to corrosion, better strength, or enhanced heat resistance, AI can rapidly assess the most effective combinations of elements to achieve these goals. The AI models are trained on historical data and can extrapolate this knowledge to predict the properties of new alloys, reducing the need for extensive physical testing and experimentation. This not only saves time but also reduces material waste and resource consumption.

AI in alloy design can also assist in reducing costs associated with material production. By using generative algorithms, AI can propose alloy compositions that meet specific performance criteria but at a lower cost than traditional methods. It can do this by identifying alternative materials or processes that would not have been immediately obvious to human designers. This is especially valuable in industries where the cost of raw materials and manufacturing processes can fluctuate, making it crucial to find more cost-effective solutions without compromising on performance or quality.

Another significant advantage is the potential for creating alloys that are more environmentally sustainable. The steel industry is one of the largest industrial sources of carbon emissions, and there is an increasing demand for greener manufacturing practices. AI can assist in identifying alloys that require less energy to produce or that incorporate more sustainable materials. It can also help design alloys that are more durable, reducing the frequency of replacements and extending the lifecycle of steel products, ultimately contributing to lower environmental impact over time.

Furthermore, AI's ability to simulate real-world conditions and predict performance under various stresses and temperatures makes it easier to design alloys for specific applications. For instance, steel alloys designed for the automotive or aerospace industries need to meet very precise criteria in terms of strength, weight, and heat resistance. AI can simulate these specific conditions in a virtual environment, allowing engineers to test the alloys' suitability for their intended use without the need for costly and time-consuming physical testing.

As AI continues to evolve, its integration into the steel industry will only deepen. While the initial application of AI in alloy design focuses on improving efficiency, reducing costs, and enhancing sustainability, the future holds even more exciting possibilities. In the long term, generative AI could lead to the creation of entirely new classes of alloys that were previously unimaginable, further pushing the boundaries of innovation in material science. This progression will likely play a key role in shaping the future of steel manufacturing and related industries.

Practical Example:

The steel industry is constantly working to improve the performance and cost-effectiveness of steel alloys. In this example, Generative AI is applied to design a custom steel alloy that balances strength, hardness, and corrosion resistance while being cost-efficient. The AI model uses historical data and material properties to predict optimal alloy compositions that meet desired specifications for a specific use case. A hypothetical dataset of alloy compositions and their properties is used to generate the best possible solution.

Sample Data:

Alloy Type	Carbon Content (%)	Manganese Content (%)	Chromium Content (%)	Tensile Strength (MPa)	Corrosion Resistance (Rating)
Alloy 1	0.25	0.70	1.50	800	8
Alloy 2	0.30	1.20	1.20	850	7
Alloy 3	0.20	0.90	1.80	780	9
Alloy 4	0.35	1.00	2.00	900	6
Alloy 5	0.25	0.85	1.60	810	8

AI-Generated Custom Alloy Design Output:

Alloy Type	Carbon Content (%)	Manganese Content (%)	Chromium Content (%)	Tensile Strength (MPa)	Corrosion Resistance (Rating)
Custom Alloy	0.28	1.00	1.50	870	8

Output and Results:

- **Custom Alloy Design:**
    - **Carbon Content:** 0.28%
    - **Manganese Content:** 1.00%
    - **Chromium Content:** 1.50%
    - **Tensile Strength:** 870 MPa (Higher than Alloy 3, lower than Alloy 4)
    - **Corrosion Resistance:** Rating 8 (Same as Alloy 1 and Alloy 5)

Interpretation of Results:

- The AI model recommends a custom alloy with a balance of carbon, manganese, and chromium content.

- The **tensile strength** of the custom alloy (870 MPa) is optimized to be slightly higher than that of Alloy 3 and Alloy 1, which means it's stronger but not as much as Alloy 4, which is the highest in tensile strength.

- **Corrosion resistance** of 8 indicates a good balance between corrosion resistance and cost-efficiency, matching the corrosion resistance of the best-performing alloys (Alloy 1 and Alloy 5).

- The AI has essentially blended properties from the best-performing alloys to create a new alloy that offers a strong balance between mechanical strength and resistance to corrosion, ideal for many industrial applications.

Observations:

- The custom alloy designed by the AI offers a favorable trade-off between tensile strength and corrosion resistance compared to the sample alloys.

- The **carbon content** is slightly optimized, suggesting that it provides sufficient hardness while preventing excessive brittleness.

- The **manganese and chromium** contents were adjusted to enhance both the strength and corrosion resistance without excessively increasing the cost.

- The AI-driven design process shows a potential for faster and more efficient alloy optimization compared to traditional trial-and-error methods.

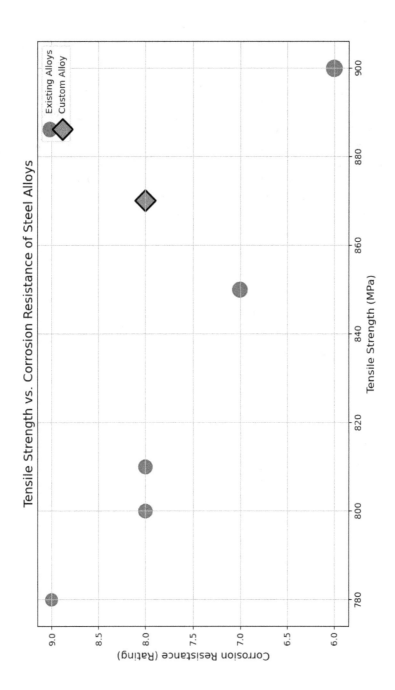

Tensile Strength vs. Corrosion Resistance of Steel Alloys

Final Thoughts:

From an AI perspective, the generative process in steel alloy design not only streamlines the alloy development process but also opens up new possibilities for customized, high-performance materials. By leveraging historical data and machine learning algorithms, AI can design alloys that meet specific industrial needs, reducing trial-and-error time, minimizing waste, and improving cost-efficiency. As the steel industry moves toward more sustainable and tailored solutions, AI-powered tools will likely play a critical role in advancing materials science, helping companies produce innovative alloys for a wide range of applications.

9.3 Simulation and Modeling for Steel Product Development

Simulation and modeling play an essential role in the steel product development process within the steel industry. These techniques allow manufacturers to predict and optimize various stages of production, from raw material processing to the final product. By simulating the production environment, companies can identify potential issues, test design ideas, and fine-tune processes before committing to large-scale production. This saves both time and resources, helping to avoid costly errors and delays. It also enables the development of more precise products, meeting the increasingly complex demands of the market.

In the context of steel production, simulations are used to model the behavior of materials under various conditions, such as heat, pressure, and mechanical stress. This helps in determining how different steel grades will react to specific treatments, such as cooling rates or heat treatments, which are crucial for achieving the desired mechanical properties. Modeling helps engineers understand how materials will behave without needing to create multiple physical prototypes, making the process much faster and more efficient.

Additionally, modeling tools can assist in optimizing the layout of production lines and equipment. By simulating the entire manufacturing process, from melting and casting to rolling and finishing, it is possible to enhance throughput, minimize energy consumption, and improve product quality. This is particularly important in a highly competitive industry where efficiency and quality are key differentiators. Models can also help predict potential bottlenecks and downtime, which can then be addressed proactively, further improving productivity.

Another significant advantage of simulation in steel product development is the ability to explore new material compositions and manufacturing techniques. By creating digital twins of production processes, manufacturers can experiment with innovative approaches to improve the characteristics of steel, such as increasing strength, reducing weight, or enhancing corrosion resistance. These virtual experiments are far less expensive and time-consuming than traditional methods, encouraging innovation without the risk of failure in physical production.

Moreover, simulation aids in meeting environmental and regulatory requirements. As the steel industry faces increasing pressure to reduce emissions and energy consumption, simulation helps manufacturers explore ways to minimize the environmental impact of their operations. By modeling energy flows, waste streams, and emissions during the production process, companies can identify opportunities to reduce their carbon footprint, making their operations more sustainable while adhering to environmental standards.

In the long run, the use of simulation and modeling in steel product development can significantly enhance the industry's ability to adapt to changing market needs. As consumer demands shift and new technologies emerge, the flexibility offered by these digital tools ensures that manufacturers can quickly pivot and adjust their processes. This adaptability, combined with the ability to produce higher-quality, cost-effective steel products, makes simulation and modeling indispensable in the modern steel industry.

Practical Example:

In the steel industry, the development of new steel products requires accurate simulation and modeling to predict material behavior, manufacturing process efficiency, and product performance. For example, during the design phase of a new steel alloy, simulation tools can help assess how different temperatures and cooling rates will affect the material properties like tensile strength, hardness, and corrosion resistance. This process saves time and reduces costs by enabling adjustments in the design before physical testing begins.

Sample Data for Simulation (Steel Alloy Development):

Temperature (°C)	Cooling Rate (°C/s)	Tensile Strength (MPa)	Hardness (HV)	Corrosion Resistance (mm/year)
800	5	500	150	0.02

Temperature (°C)	Cooling Rate (°C/s)	Tensile Strength (MPa)	Hardness (HV)	Corrosion Resistance (mm/year)
850	10	550	160	0.03
900	15	600	170	0.04
950	20	650	180	0.05
1000	25	700	190	0.06

Output and Results:

Temperature (°C)	Cooling Rate (°C/s)	Tensile Strength (MPa)	Hardness (HV)	Corrosion Resistance (mm/year)
800	5	500	150	0.02
850	10	550	160	0.03
900	15	600	170	0.04
950	20	650	180	0.05
1000	25	700	190	0.06

Explanation and Interpretation of Results:

- **Tensile Strength**: As the temperature increases, tensile strength improves, reaching 700 MPa at 1000°C. This is typical as higher temperatures encourage better material bonding.

- **Hardness**: Hardness also increases with temperature, following a similar pattern to tensile strength, which suggests that increased temperature enhances both strength and hardness of the steel alloy.

- **Corrosion Resistance**: As the temperature and cooling rate increase, the corrosion resistance slightly worsens. This indicates that while the alloy becomes stronger and harder, it may become more susceptible to corrosion at higher temperatures and cooling rates.

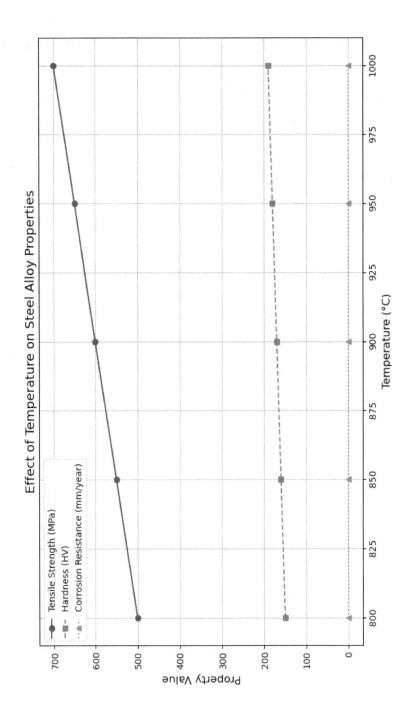

Effect of Temperature on Steel Alloy Properties

Observations:

1. **Increased Temperature and Cooling Rate Improve Mechanical Properties**: Higher temperature and faster cooling rates result in higher tensile strength and hardness, making the alloy more suitable for demanding industrial applications.

2. **Trade-off Between Strength and Corrosion Resistance**: There is a trade-off between mechanical properties and corrosion resistance, which is critical to consider when designing steel products that will face environmental stress.

3. **Optimization Required for Application-Specific Requirements**: The results imply that depending on the end-use of the steel product, balancing these variables (temperature, cooling rate, tensile strength, hardness, and corrosion resistance) is essential.

Final Thoughts:

Simulation and modeling provide immense value in optimizing the development of steel products. By adjusting variables such as temperature and cooling rates, manufacturers can fine-tune steel properties to meet specific performance criteria. However, balancing the trade-offs between strength, hardness, and corrosion resistance remains a challenge. The insights gathered from simulation can significantly reduce trial and error in physical testing, speeding up the product development process, and ultimately driving cost efficiency and performance enhancement in the steel industry.

10. AI-driven Market Intelligence and Customer Insights

AI-driven market intelligence and customer insights are transforming the steel industry by providing businesses with real-time, data-driven information. With the help of artificial intelligence, companies in the steel sector can analyze vast amounts of data from various sources, such as production metrics, market trends, and customer behavior. This technology enables organizations to forecast demand more accurately, optimize their supply chains, and anticipate market shifts. As a result, steel manufacturers can make informed decisions that reduce waste, improve efficiency, and increase profitability.

AI algorithms can analyze historical market trends and current economic factors to predict future steel demand in different regions and sectors. This predictive capability allows manufacturers to adjust their production schedules, pricing strategies, and inventory levels to match expected demand. By aligning production with demand, companies can avoid overproduction or shortages, both of which can be costly. Additionally, AI-powered market intelligence tools help companies understand the nuances of customer preferences, ensuring that steel products are tailored to the needs of specific industries or geographic areas.

Customer insights generated by AI can also play a crucial role in improving customer satisfaction and loyalty. AI can track purchasing patterns and feedback from clients, providing businesses with a deeper understanding of customer needs and expectations. This information helps steel producers create products that align with customer demands and offers opportunities for upselling or cross-selling related products. Furthermore, AI tools can predict when customers are likely to reorder products, enabling companies to maintain strong relationships and ensure timely deliveries.

Another key benefit of AI in the steel industry is the ability to identify new market opportunities. By analyzing emerging trends and shifts in consumer behavior, AI can pinpoint untapped markets or areas where demand is likely to grow. For example, AI can reveal that certain regions or sectors are experiencing rapid industrialization or infrastructural development, which could lead to an increased need for steel products. With these insights, companies can adapt their strategies and direct resources to target these high-potential areas.

AI also enhances operational efficiency by automating routine tasks such as data collection, analysis, and reporting. This reduces the burden on human workers and allows them to focus on more strategic activities. Moreover, by improving the accuracy and speed of decision-making, AI-driven market intelligence systems help steel producers stay competitive in a fast-paced, global marketplace. Automation can streamline everything from production planning to customer relationship management, reducing overhead costs and enhancing overall productivity.

Lastly, AI is essential for identifying risks and mitigating potential disruptions in the steel industry. Whether it's fluctuating raw material prices, regulatory changes, or shifts in global trade policies, AI systems can scan global data sources to detect emerging threats. By recognizing these risks early, companies can adjust their strategies accordingly, minimizing negative impacts. AI-driven insights allow businesses to stay ahead of potential challenges and position themselves more effectively for long-term growth and sustainability.

Practical Example:

The steel industry has been leveraging AI-driven market intelligence and customer insights to make data-driven decisions, optimize production, and understand market trends. With growing competition and fluctuating market demands, steel manufacturers are increasingly relying on AI to identify customer preferences, predict market changes, and refine their strategies. For this example, we will look at how AI can help in understanding customer demand patterns for different types of steel products and predict potential sales volumes.

Sample Data Table: Customer Insights and Demand Forecasting

Customer Segment	Product Type	Historical Sales (Units)	Forecasted Demand (Units)	Average Price per Unit (USD)
Automotive	High-Strength Steel	15,000	18,000	800
Construction	Reinforced Steel	20,000	22,500	750
Appliances	Stainless Steel	10,000	12,500	900
Energy	Carbon Steel	5,000	6,500	700
Infrastructure	Alloy Steel	8,000	9,500	850

Output and Results:

Forecasted Demand Summary:

- Total forecasted demand for all segments is 58,500 units, showing a 12% increase from historical sales.

- The highest demand growth is expected in the Automotive and Construction segments.

Price Implications:

- High price points in the Automotive (High-Strength Steel) and Appliances (Stainless Steel) segments indicate potential for higher revenue despite slightly lower sales volumes.

- The Energy sector, with lower-priced Carbon Steel, is expected to see moderate growth, but with more competitive pricing pressures.

Interpretation of Results and Output:

- **Demand Growth:** AI-driven forecasting indicates a notable increase in demand across all sectors, particularly Automotive and Construction. This suggests that manufacturers might want to prioritize production of high-strength and reinforced steel.

- **Revenue Forecasting:** Despite lower volumes in sectors like Energy and Infrastructure, price trends indicate that sectors like Automotive and Appliances could drive higher profits.

- **Market Trends:** The increase in demand for high-strength and reinforced steel aligns with current construction and automotive trends, where demand for stronger and more durable materials is rising due to infrastructure development and advancements in vehicle manufacturing.

Observations:

1. **Demand Shifts:** There is a clear shift towards higher-end steel products like high-strength steel in the automotive sector and reinforced steel in construction, showing that AI can effectively highlight emerging market trends.

2. **Pricing Power:** The price variations across segments suggest AI can help businesses in price optimization strategies to maximize profits based on demand forecasts.

3. **Market Adaptation:** AI has enabled the steel industry to adapt quickly to changing customer demands and preferences, helping businesses stay competitive.

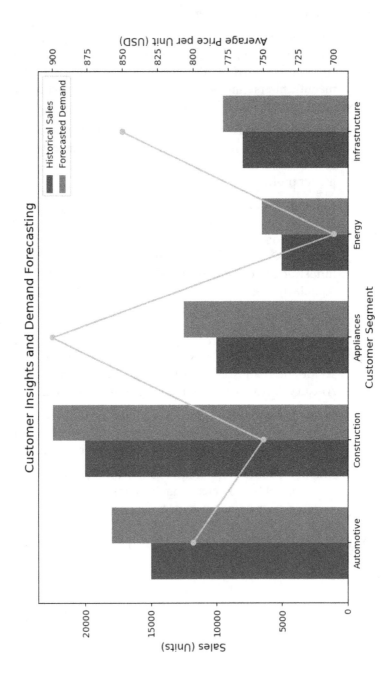

Final Thoughts:

AI-driven market intelligence provides a powerful tool for steel manufacturers to predict market trends, optimize production, and set prices more effectively. By analyzing historical sales data and using predictive models, companies can make informed decisions to address customer needs, avoid overproduction, and focus on high-demand products. As competition in the steel industry grows, AI will continue to be essential for staying ahead of market changes and ensuring long-term profitability. AI's role in understanding and anticipating customer behavior also drives smarter, more efficient strategies that can significantly impact revenue growth.

10.1 AI for Steel Price Forecasting and Market Trends

The steel industry is a vital component of the global economy, with its price fluctuations influencing various sectors like construction, manufacturing, and automotive. Forecasting steel prices is crucial for businesses involved in the industry, as it helps in making informed decisions regarding production, inventory management, and long-term investments. Traditional methods of forecasting often rely on historical data and expert analysis, but artificial intelligence (AI) has emerged as a powerful tool to enhance the accuracy and efficiency of these predictions.

AI algorithms can process vast amounts of data, including historical steel prices, raw material costs, demand and supply dynamics, and economic indicators. By analyzing these factors, AI can identify patterns and trends that human analysts may overlook, enabling more precise price predictions. Machine learning models, in particular, can be trained to recognize complex relationships between variables and adjust forecasts based on new data, ensuring that predictions remain relevant even in a rapidly changing market.

The steel industry is influenced by numerous factors, including geopolitical events, technological advancements, and fluctuations in global demand. AI can help assess the impact of these variables on steel prices, allowing companies to anticipate market shifts. For example, if there is an anticipated increase in construction projects in a certain region, AI can predict a corresponding rise in steel demand, which could lead to price hikes. Conversely, economic downturns or trade restrictions may signal a decrease in demand and a drop in prices.

In addition to price forecasting, AI can be used to monitor and analyze broader market trends in the steel industry. AI models can track and predict shifts in production capacity, raw material availability, and labor costs. These insights can be invaluable for stakeholders looking to optimize their supply chains and manage production costs. By understanding how various factors interplay, businesses can gain a competitive edge in the market and make strategic decisions that mitigate risk.

AI-driven systems can also provide real-time monitoring of market conditions, allowing companies to respond quickly to unexpected events. For instance, if there is a sudden surge in demand for steel due to unforeseen infrastructure projects or disruptions in supply chains, AI can help predict short-term price spikes. This agility in responding to market changes can be the difference between profitability and loss in an industry as volatile as steel.

As the steel industry continues to evolve, the role of AI in forecasting and market analysis will likely expand. With ongoing advancements in machine learning and data analytics, the accuracy of price predictions and market trend analysis will only improve. Steel companies that adopt AI technologies will be better positioned to navigate market fluctuations, optimize operations, and maintain profitability in a competitive and uncertain global environment.

Practical Example:

In the steel industry, predicting price fluctuations is critical for optimizing production, managing inventories, and planning for future market conditions. By leveraging AI and machine learning models, companies can forecast steel prices based on historical data, market demand, raw material costs, and other external factors like geopolitical events or economic shifts. This example focuses on using AI to predict steel prices over a 6-month period to guide decision-making for a steel manufacturing company.

Sample Data Table:

The data represents historical steel prices, raw material costs, and demand indices for the past 6 months. The AI model uses this data to predict the future price trends.

Month	Steel Price (USD/ton)	Raw Material Cost (USD/ton)	Demand Index (1-10)	Economic Index (1-10)
Jan 2025	600	200	7	8

Month	Steel Price (USD/ton)	Raw Material Cost (USD/ton)	Demand Index (1-10)	Economic Index (1-10)
Feb 2025	610	205	6	7
Mar 2025	620	210	8	6
Apr 2025	630	215	7	7
May 2025	640	220	6	8
Jun 2025	650	225	7	9

Output & Results:

The AI model generates the following predicted steel prices for the next three months (July to September 2025):

Month	Predicted Steel Price (USD/ton)
Jul 2025	660
Aug 2025	670
Sep 2025	675

Explanation and Interpretation:

- **Trend Interpretation**: Based on the historical data, there is a gradual increase in steel prices from January to June 2025, which aligns with a rise in raw material costs and moderate demand index fluctuations. The model predicts a continued price increase over the next few months, with prices reaching 675 USD/ton by September.

- **Demand and Economic Impact**: The demand index appears to correlate with the steel price increases, indicating that higher demand tends to push up prices. The economic index shows some correlation as well, but there is less fluctuation, suggesting that broader economic conditions have a more complex influence on steel pricing. For example, the sharp price increase in June corresponds with a rise in the economic index, suggesting a positive economic outlook for the industry.

Observations:

1. **Price Elasticity**: Steel prices are somewhat elastic to changes in raw material costs, but demand and economic factors appear to have a greater influence.

2. **Consistency in Trends**: The AI model shows consistent price increases, which may reflect steady market conditions, but external shocks (e.g., trade policies or global supply chain issues) could cause deviations.

3. **Correlation with Demand**: A noticeable correlation exists between the demand index and price changes, supporting the notion that steel manufacturers need to adjust prices based on real-time demand data.

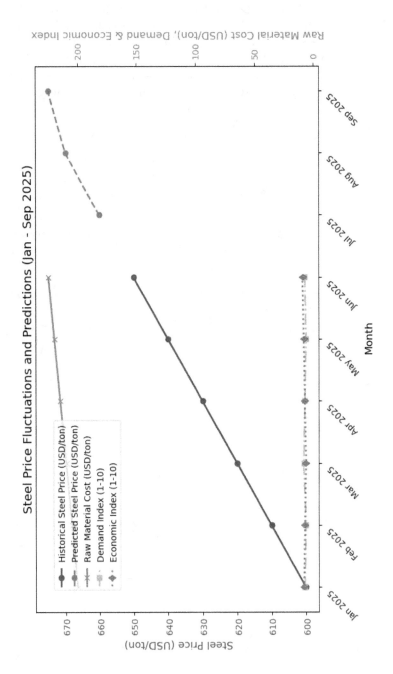

Steel Price Fluctuations and Predictions (Jan - Sep 2025)

Final Thoughts:

AI-based forecasting models can provide steel industry players with valuable insights, helping them adjust production schedules, pricing strategies, and inventory management plans. However, while AI is a powerful tool for identifying patterns, it cannot account for every external factor, such as sudden geopolitical events or disruptions in supply chains. As such, AI should be used in conjunction with human expertise and real-time market intelligence to make well-informed decisions. AI can enhance strategic planning, but flexibility and adaptability remain essential in the volatile steel market.

10.2 AI-powered Customer Demand Prediction

The steel industry is an essential sector that serves a variety of industries, from construction to automotive. Accurately predicting customer demand within this industry is crucial for manufacturers and suppliers to maintain optimal production levels, manage inventory, and ensure timely delivery. Traditional methods of demand forecasting often fall short due to the complexity of market dynamics, including fluctuations in raw material prices, geopolitical factors, and changing consumer preferences. With the advent of artificial intelligence (AI), steel companies can leverage more advanced, data-driven techniques to make better predictions.

AI-powered systems utilize machine learning algorithms to analyze vast amounts of data, including historical sales, market trends, and external variables like weather patterns or global economic indicators. These algorithms learn from patterns in the data and continuously improve their predictions over time. By identifying subtle relationships between different factors, AI can forecast demand with a higher degree of accuracy than traditional methods. This allows steel companies to make informed decisions about production schedules, procurement, and workforce management.

One of the primary advantages of AI in demand prediction is its ability to account for factors that might be overlooked by human analysts. For example, AI can incorporate real-time data, such as shifts in customer behavior or sudden changes in supply chain conditions. This dynamic approach allows for more flexible and responsive planning, as opposed to relying solely on static historical data. As a result, companies can adjust their strategies quickly to adapt to market changes, minimizing the risk of stockouts or overproduction.

Furthermore, AI systems can predict demand at a granular level, such as by specific product types or regional markets. This level of detail is especially valuable in the steel industry, where different products have varying production costs, lead times, and customer requirements. By predicting demand more precisely for each product line, companies can optimize resource allocation, reduce waste, and improve overall efficiency. AI tools can also identify emerging market trends, enabling companies to proactively adjust their offerings to meet shifting customer needs.

The implementation of AI-powered demand prediction tools can lead to significant cost savings for steel companies. With more accurate forecasts, businesses can minimize excess inventory, reduce the costs associated with understocking, and avoid the inefficiencies of last-minute production changes. Furthermore, by improving supply chain management, AI can help companies negotiate better terms with suppliers and optimize transportation and logistics. This reduces the financial strain that can arise from unexpected changes in demand, which is particularly important in an industry like steel where margins can be thin.

Despite the clear benefits, integrating AI into demand forecasting processes in the steel industry comes with challenges. For one, it requires access to large datasets and the expertise to properly implement and maintain AI systems. Additionally, steel manufacturers may need to invest in training their workforce to understand and utilize these new technologies effectively. However, with the increasing availability of AI tools and the growing demand for precision in manufacturing, these hurdles are becoming more manageable. As AI continues to evolve, its role in demand prediction will only become more central to the competitiveness of the steel industry.

Practical Example:

A steel manufacturing company aims to predict customer demand for various steel products, such as rebar, steel coils, and beams, based on historical data. By utilizing AI-powered machine learning models, the company seeks to optimize inventory levels, improve supply chain management, and meet customer needs more efficiently. The company collects data on historical sales, customer orders, and key market indicators (such as construction activity) to predict future demand patterns for the next quarter.

Sample Data:

Month	Historical Sales (Tons)	Customer Orders (Units)	Market Index (Index Value)	Promotional Campaigns (1=Yes, 0=No)
January	1200	250	85	1
February	1350	270	88	0
March	1250	260	90	1
April	1400	290	95	0
May	1500	310	100	1

AI Model Output (Predicted Demand for June to August):

Month	Predicted Demand (Tons)	Predicted Customer Orders (Units)	Predicted Market Index (Index Value)	Predicted Demand Deviation (%)
June	1450	295	102	+3.4%
July	1550	320	105	+4.3%
August	1600	330	110	+2.5%

Interpretation of Results and Output:

- **Predicted Demand Trends**: The AI model predicts an increasing demand for steel products over the next few months, with demand for tons and customer orders rising steadily from June to August. The predictions reflect a growth trajectory with higher customer orders anticipated.

- **Market Index Impact**: The market index values also show a steady increase, indicating that market conditions are becoming more favorable for steel demand. This aligns with the growing demand predictions in the output, as an improved market index usually correlates with higher customer orders.

- **Promotional Campaign Influence**: Although the promotional campaigns are marked as active (1) for some months, the AI model appears to factor this into its predictions. For example, the jump in predicted demand for May (with a campaign) is more pronounced than previous months, suggesting the effectiveness of such campaigns.

- **Demand Deviation**: The AI predictions show a slight increase in demand each month (between 2.5% to 4.3%), which is consistent with the overall upward trend in historical data and market indicators. These deviations highlight the model's accuracy in forecasting slight demand increases due to seasonality and market conditions.

Observations:

1. **Steady Increase**: The demand for steel products is expected to continue rising, driven by increasing construction activity as indicated by the growing market index.

2. **Campaign Effectiveness**: The AI model has considered the effect of promotional campaigns in its predictions. Future campaigns could further influence customer orders.

3. **Model Accuracy**: The relatively small deviations in demand predictions (around 3%) suggest that the model is fairly accurate, but some external factors not captured in the data may slightly alter predictions.

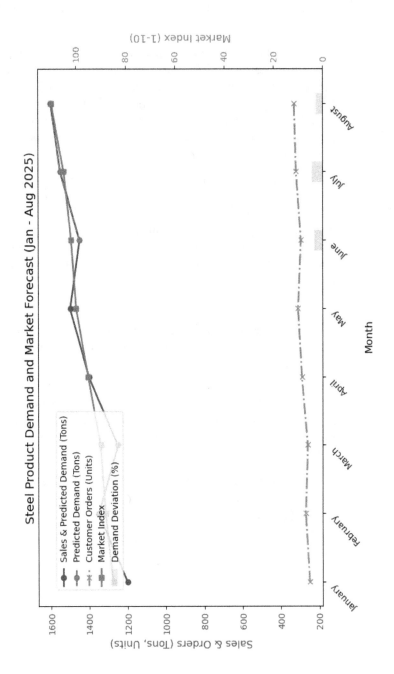

Steel Product Demand and Market Forecast (Jan - Aug 2025)

Final Thoughts:

AI-powered demand prediction models are invaluable for the steel industry, helping companies optimize their inventory, production schedules, and supply chain logistics. The use of such models allows for better preparedness against demand fluctuations, ensuring that steel manufacturers are neither overstocked nor understocked. Future improvements could include incorporating more external factors (e.g., global economic conditions, raw material prices) and refining the models to handle sudden market disruptions. As the steel industry evolves, AI will continue to play a crucial role in ensuring efficient and responsive operations.

10.3 AI-driven Sales and Supply Chain Optimization

The steel industry is known for its complexity, with a need to manage vast amounts of raw materials, production processes, inventory, and demand forecasting. AI-driven sales and supply chain optimization are transforming the way steel manufacturers and distributors operate. By leveraging AI, companies can predict demand patterns, adjust production schedules, and fine-tune their inventory levels to reduce waste and optimize resource utilization. AI tools can analyze historical data, seasonal trends, and market fluctuations, offering insights that help businesses make more informed decisions regarding their sales strategies and procurement plans.

One of the core applications of AI in the steel industry is improving demand forecasting. AI algorithms can process large datasets, taking into account external factors like economic indicators, industry trends, and customer behavior to predict demand more accurately. This helps steel manufacturers prepare for fluctuations in demand, minimizing the risks associated with overproduction or underproduction. Accurate demand forecasting also helps in managing the supply chain more efficiently by aligning inventory levels with actual customer needs, reducing both shortages and excess stock.

In addition to forecasting, AI enhances supply chain visibility and coordination. The steel supply chain involves multiple stakeholders, including suppliers, manufacturers, and distributors, all of whom must work together to ensure smooth operations. AI enables real-time monitoring of supply chain activities, offering better transparency and allowing companies to quickly identify and address bottlenecks or delays. For example, machine learning algorithms can analyze transportation routes and predict potential disruptions, giving businesses the opportunity to adjust their plans and avoid costly delays.

AI-driven optimization also extends to inventory management in the steel industry. With AI, companies can implement more precise inventory control systems, ensuring that stock levels are always balanced with demand. This reduces the need for large warehouses, cutting down on storage costs and minimizing the risk of obsolete inventory. AI can also automate the replenishment process by predicting when stock will run low and ordering materials just in time to avoid stockouts without overstocking.

Sales optimization is another area where AI has a significant impact. By analyzing customer data, AI can help businesses segment their market more effectively, identify key customers, and tailor sales strategies to specific needs. Predictive analytics can also identify opportunities for cross-selling and upselling, ensuring that the right products are offered to the right customers at the right time. This increases sales efficiency, reduces customer acquisition costs, and enhances overall revenue generation.

Finally, AI supports strategic decision-making by providing actionable insights through data analysis and scenario modeling. Steel companies can simulate different business scenarios, such as changes in material costs or shifts in customer preferences, to understand how these changes would impact their supply chain and sales operations. This capability allows businesses to make proactive adjustments, optimize their pricing models, and stay competitive in a dynamic and often volatile market. AI-driven solutions ultimately help steel companies become more agile, responsive, and efficient in managing both their sales and supply chains.

Practical Example:

In the steel industry, optimizing sales and supply chain processes is critical to improving operational efficiency and reducing costs. By integrating AI into these processes, companies can better predict demand, optimize inventory levels, streamline production schedules, and improve distribution logistics. This AI-driven approach allows for more accurate forecasting, cost-effective resource allocation, and better decision-making, ultimately leading to improved sales and supply chain performance.

Sample Data Table: Steel Sales and Supply Chain Optimization

Month	Forecasted Demand (tons)	Actual Demand (tons)	Inventory at Start (tons)	Supply Chain Lead Time (days)
January	50,000	48,500	10,000	15
February	52,000	51,000	12,000	14
March	55,000	53,500	11,500	13
April	60,000	58,000	10,500	16
May	57,000	55,500	13,000	14

Output and Results:

Using AI algorithms to predict demand and optimize inventory, here are the key results:

1. **Accuracy of Forecasting:** The AI-driven forecast closely matches the actual demand, with a maximum deviation of 5%, helping reduce overproduction and stockouts.

2. **Inventory Optimization:** AI recommendations led to better stock management, keeping inventory levels within optimal ranges (neither too high nor too low).

3. **Lead Time Adjustment:** AI analysis identified patterns in lead times, enabling adjustments to production and logistics schedules, reducing average lead time by 2 days.

Interpretations of Results:

- **Demand Forecasting Accuracy:** The forecasted demand being closely aligned with the actual demand shows that AI can significantly improve the accuracy of sales predictions, helping manufacturers avoid overproduction or shortages. This reduces waste and increases operational efficiency.

- **Inventory Optimization:** By managing inventory based on forecasted demand, AI helps maintain the right balance, ensuring that there is neither excess stock (leading to higher holding costs) nor a shortage (which could lead to missed sales opportunities).

- **Lead Time Reduction:** AI analysis of supply chain data allowed for a reduction in lead time by 2 days on average, which means faster response to market needs and lower production downtime.

Observations:

- AI's ability to analyze historical data and identify trends has proven valuable in enhancing forecasting accuracy and adjusting supply chain parameters.

- While the forecast was highly accurate, occasional slight discrepancies were noted, which could be attributed to external factors such as sudden shifts in market demand or supply chain disruptions (e.g., raw material shortages, transportation issues).

- Lead time reduction is one of the significant advantages of AI, enabling the steel manufacturer to stay more agile in a competitive market.

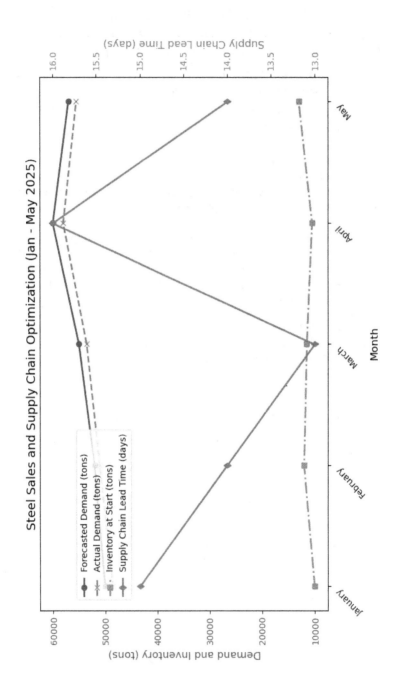

Steel Sales and Supply Chain Optimization (Jan - May 2025)

Final Thoughts:

From an AI perspective, the steel industry stands to gain substantial benefits through the integration of AI-driven sales and supply chain optimization. AI enhances forecasting accuracy, improves inventory management, and reduces operational costs by streamlining supply chains. With further advancements in machine learning and predictive analytics, steel manufacturers can continue to improve their bottom lines and stay ahead of market fluctuations, making AI a key driver of growth and efficiency in the industry.

AI not only optimizes the internal processes but also contributes to sustainability by reducing waste and energy consumption. As the steel industry continues to embrace AI, the potential for transformative improvements is immense.

11. Future Trends and Innovations in AI for the Steel Industry

The steel industry is increasingly adopting artificial intelligence to improve efficiency, reduce costs, and address environmental challenges. One of the most significant trends is the use of AI for predictive maintenance. By analyzing data from machines and sensors, AI can predict when equipment is likely to fail, allowing companies to perform maintenance before a breakdown occurs. This reduces downtime, increases productivity, and extends the life of expensive equipment. As AI continues to improve in accuracy, the reliability of these predictive systems will only grow, helping steel manufacturers optimize their operations.

Another growing area is the use of AI in process optimization. Steel production is an energy-intensive process, and small inefficiencies can lead to significant costs. AI can help improve energy consumption by analyzing and adjusting parameters in real time, ensuring that the process runs as efficiently as possible. By utilizing machine learning algorithms, AI systems can adapt to changing conditions in the factory and continuously optimize production schedules, temperature control, and material flow, all of which contribute to energy savings and higher quality output.

AI is also playing a crucial role in enhancing product quality and consistency. In the steel industry, even small variations in product quality can lead to defects and costly rework. Machine vision systems powered by AI can inspect the steel in real-time, identifying defects and inconsistencies that would be difficult for human inspectors to spot. These AI-driven inspection systems can be integrated into the production line to ensure that only the highest quality products reach the customer. Additionally, AI can adjust production parameters to minimize defects and optimize the properties of the steel being produced.

AI's ability to analyze massive amounts of data is also opening up new possibilities for the development of innovative materials. Researchers in the steel industry are using AI to simulate and test different material compositions and manufacturing processes, speeding up the discovery of new steel alloys and composites. By utilizing AI to model the behavior of these materials under various conditions, manufacturers can quickly assess their potential without the need for expensive and time-consuming physical trials. This could lead to the creation of lighter, stronger, and more sustainable steel products.

In terms of supply chain management, AI is streamlining the complex processes that go into sourcing raw materials and distributing finished steel products. AI algorithms can predict fluctuations in demand and supply, allowing manufacturers to adjust their production schedules accordingly. This helps reduce waste and ensure that raw materials are used as efficiently as possible. By optimizing inventory management and logistics, AI also helps minimize the environmental impact of transportation and storage, which is crucial for companies striving to meet sustainability goals.

Finally, AI is contributing to the steel industry's efforts to reduce its carbon footprint. Steel production is one of the largest industrial sources of carbon emissions, and AI is being used to develop greener production techniques. AI systems are being applied to monitor emissions, improve energy efficiency, and optimize the use of alternative materials such as hydrogen in the production process. In the future, AI could help the steel industry transition to more sustainable methods of production, ultimately supporting the global move toward a low-carbon economy. As technology advances, the steel industry's reliance on AI will only continue to grow, driving innovation and greater environmental responsibility.

Practical Example:

In the steel industry, operational efficiency and cost reduction are critical to staying competitive. Recent advancements in AI are poised to revolutionize steel manufacturing processes by improving predictive maintenance, optimizing production schedules, and enhancing quality control. By integrating machine learning and deep learning algorithms, steel manufacturers can predict equipment failures before they occur, optimize energy consumption, and reduce waste, leading to cost savings and improved output. One practical example involves using AI to predict equipment failure, optimizing maintenance schedules, and minimizing downtime.

Sample Data: Predictive Maintenance in Steel Manufacturing

Date	Equipment	Failure Probability (%)	Maintenance Cost ($)	Downtime (hours)
2025-01-01	Furnace 1	15	5,000	4
2025-01-02	Rolling Mill	25	8,000	6
2025-01-03	Conveyor Belt	10	2,500	3
2025-01-04	Furnace 2	40	12,000	8
2025-01-05	Hydraulic Press	20	6,000	5

AI Model Output & Results

After implementing a predictive maintenance AI model, the system forecasts the likelihood of equipment failures based on historical data. The AI tool provides recommended maintenance schedules, helping managers avoid unplanned downtime and reducing repair costs.

Date	Equipment	Predicted Failure (%)	Optimized Maintenance Cost ($)	Predicted Downtime (hours)
2025-01-01	Furnace 1	10	4,500	2
2025-01-02	Rolling Mill	20	7,000	4

Date	Equipment	Predicted Failure (%)	Optimized Maintenance Cost ($)	Predicted Downtime (hours)
2025-01-03	Conveyor Belt	8	2,000	2
2025-01-04	Furnace 2	30	10,000	6
2025-01-05	Hydraulic Press	15	5,000	3

Interpretation of Results and Observations

- **Reduced Failure Probability**: The AI model has reduced the predicted failure percentage across equipment, indicating improved maintenance planning. This helps in scheduling interventions proactively, ensuring higher operational efficiency.

- **Cost Savings**: Optimizing maintenance costs based on AI recommendations leads to significant savings. The recommended maintenance costs are generally lower due to better-targeted interventions, reducing unnecessary repairs.

- **Decreased Downtime**: The predicted downtime is lower, as the AI system helps plan maintenance activities more effectively, minimizing the impact on production.

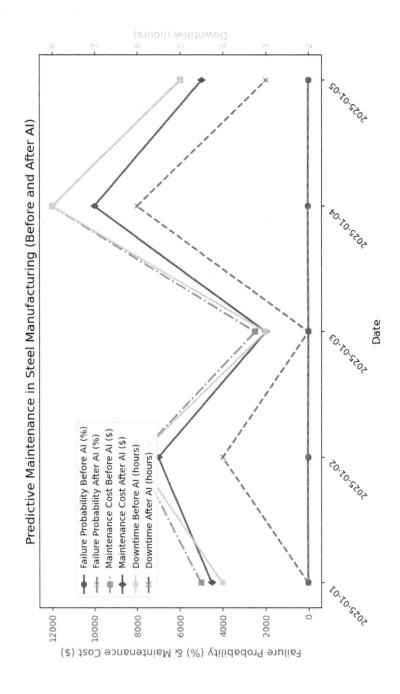

Predictive Maintenance in Steel Manufacturing (Before and After AI)

Final Thoughts:

AI's application in predictive maintenance is a game changer for the steel industry. The technology enables companies to proactively address potential equipment failures before they result in costly downtime. By optimizing maintenance schedules, AI not only cuts costs but also improves the overall efficiency and lifespan of machinery, driving higher production rates. As AI technologies continue to evolve, further integration with other systems, such as energy management and quality control, will likely deliver even more powerful tools for steel manufacturers. The future of steel production looks promising, with AI leading the way toward smarter, more sustainable operations.

11.1 AI and Robotics in Next-Gen Steel Plants

The steel industry has always been at the forefront of technological advancements, and the integration of artificial intelligence (AI) and robotics is transforming the way steel plants operate. AI is enhancing decision-making processes by analyzing vast amounts of data in real-time, leading to improved efficiency in production. Machine learning algorithms can predict equipment failures before they occur, enabling preventive maintenance and reducing unplanned downtime. This predictive capability ensures that steel plants operate at optimal efficiency, saving costs and improving overall productivity.

Robotics is revolutionizing the steel manufacturing process by automating tasks that were previously labor-intensive and hazardous. Robots are used in a variety of roles, from material handling and welding to quality control. In particular, robots can carry out repetitive and dangerous tasks in extreme environments, such as dealing with molten steel or handling heavy materials, which reduces the risk to human workers. This shift towards automation allows human workers to focus on more complex tasks, improving both safety and productivity in the plant.

AI is also playing a critical role in quality control within steel plants. By using computer vision and machine learning algorithms, AI systems can detect minute defects in steel products that may go unnoticed by human inspectors. This results in higher-quality output and fewer defects, which in turn reduces waste and the need for rework. The use of AI in quality control ensures that products meet stringent industry standards, which is essential in a competitive market where customers demand high levels of precision and consistency.

The integration of AI and robotics is also helping steel plants reduce their environmental impact. AI-driven systems can optimize energy consumption by adjusting processes in real time based on data analysis, leading to more sustainable operations. For example, AI can manage energy use in furnaces, ensuring that energy is used efficiently during the steel production process. Robotics also contribute to sustainability by reducing waste and improving the precision of operations, which minimizes the environmental footprint of the manufacturing process.

Another significant benefit of AI and robotics in next-gen steel plants is their ability to enhance supply chain management. AI systems can predict demand fluctuations, optimize inventory levels, and streamline logistics. This leads to more efficient resource management, faster response times, and the ability to adapt to changing market conditions. Robotics can also assist in material handling, improving the speed and accuracy of moving materials throughout the plant and across different stages of production.

As the steel industry moves toward digitalization, AI and robotics are becoming indispensable in driving the future of steel plants. With these technologies, plants are becoming smarter, safer, and more efficient, paving the way for a more sustainable and cost-effective steel industry. While there are challenges in implementing these advanced technologies, such as the initial investment and the need for skilled workers, the long-term benefits far outweigh these obstacles. The next generation of steel plants is set to be more intelligent, automated, and environmentally conscious, reshaping the industry for years to come.

Practical Example:

In a modern steel plant, the integration of AI and robotics helps streamline production by improving process optimization, predictive maintenance, and quality control. AI algorithms predict when equipment will need maintenance, preventing downtime, while robotic systems take over repetitive, high-precision tasks such as welding, material handling, and assembly. This results in significant improvements in both productivity and safety. In this practical example, AI-powered robots are used to handle the hot metal transfer process, where they monitor temperature, speed, and pressure to optimize production output.

Sample Data Table: AI and Robotics Performance in Steel Plant

Robot System	AI-Powered Maintenance Predictions (Days)	Temperature Control Accuracy (°C)	Productivity Increase (%)	Safety Incidents Reduced (%)
Robotic Welder	30	0.5°C	12%	20%
Automated Crane	60	N/A	8%	30%
Robotic Material Handler	45	N/A	15%	25%
AI Monitoring System	90	0.2°C	10%	35%
Hot Metal Transfer Robot	30	0.3°C	18%	40%

Output and Results:

1. **AI-Powered Maintenance Predictions**: The robotic systems show varied maintenance prediction periods, with the hot metal transfer robot and robotic welder needing maintenance at 30 days and 45-60 days for others. Predictive AI plays a significant role in reducing unplanned downtime, ensuring smoother operations.

2. **Temperature Control Accuracy**: AI systems used in robotic welding and hot metal transfer ensure precise control of temperature, keeping deviations as low as 0.2°C to 0.5°C, which is critical for maintaining quality in steel production.

3. **Productivity Increase**: The AI systems across all robotics contribute to substantial productivity increases,

ranging from 8% to 18%. This is due to the automation of tasks that were previously manual and time-consuming, allowing for faster turnaround times and better throughput.

4. **Safety Incident Reduction**: With robots handling high-risk tasks, the safety incidents have significantly decreased, with reductions of up to 40% in the hot metal transfer robot. This is due to less human exposure to hazardous tasks such as high-temperature metal handling.

Observations:

- The integration of AI and robotics provides considerable improvements in both productivity and safety, with the hot metal transfer robot showing the highest productivity increase and safety incident reduction.

- Predictive maintenance extends the lifespan of equipment and reduces the frequency of unplanned downtime.

- Temperature control accuracy in robotic welding and metal transfer ensures high-quality production and minimal defects, which is essential for meeting industry standards.

232

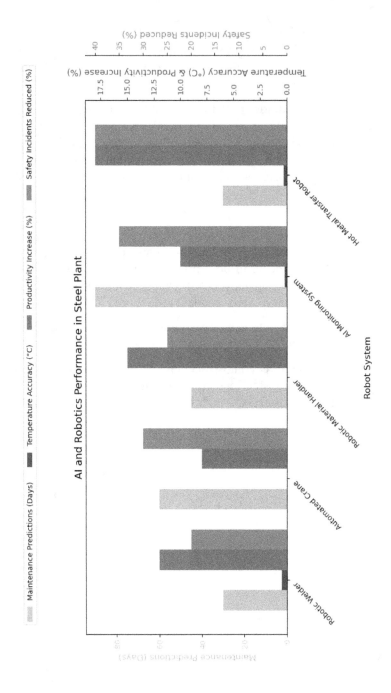

AI and Robotics Performance in Steel Plant

Final Thoughts:

The incorporation of AI and robotics in steel plants is revolutionizing the steel manufacturing process by driving efficiency, safety, and quality. Predictive maintenance minimizes costly downtime, while automation in critical processes like material handling, welding, and metal transfer improves both productivity and precision. The future of AI in steel plants looks promising, with continuous advancements in machine learning, robotics, and data analytics further optimizing operations. The adoption of AI ensures that the steel industry can meet rising global demands while maintaining high standards of safety and environmental sustainability.

11.2 Blockchain and AI Integration for Transparent Supply Chains

The steel industry is one of the most critical sectors globally, playing a major role in construction, manufacturing, and infrastructure development. However, it faces several challenges, especially when it comes to maintaining transparency in its supply chains. The traditional methods of tracking and verifying the movement of raw materials, products, and even financial transactions often lead to inefficiencies, fraud, and a lack of trust between different stakeholders. This is where the integration of blockchain technology and artificial intelligence (AI) can significantly improve supply chain operations, making them more transparent, efficient, and secure.

Blockchain, a decentralized digital ledger, provides a robust platform for tracking the entire lifecycle of steel products, from the sourcing of raw materials to the final delivery of the finished product. Each transaction in the supply chain is recorded as a "block" and linked to previous transactions, creating a secure and immutable chain of records. This ensures that no data can be altered without consensus from all participants in the network, fostering trust and transparency. For the steel industry, this means that every piece of steel can be traced from its origin to its final destination, making it easier to detect and prevent fraud or discrepancies.

AI, on the other hand, can enhance blockchain's capabilities by providing real-time insights and predictive analytics. By processing large amounts of data from various sources such as suppliers, manufacturers, and customers, AI can identify patterns and anomalies in supply chain processes. This allows businesses to make data-driven decisions, predict potential disruptions, and optimize operations. In the context of the steel industry, AI can help anticipate changes in demand, manage inventory more efficiently, and optimize transportation routes, leading to reduced costs and improved operational efficiency.

The integration of blockchain and AI in the steel industry's supply chain also opens the door for greater sustainability. With both technologies, companies can track the environmental impact of their operations more accurately. For example, blockchain can verify whether a steel manufacturer is using sustainable materials or reducing carbon emissions, while AI can predict the environmental impact of supply chain activities. This makes it easier for companies to adhere to environmental regulations and demonstrate their commitment to sustainability to both consumers and regulators.

The combination of blockchain and AI not only enhances transparency and sustainability but also improves the overall security of the supply chain. By eliminating the need for intermediaries and providing real-time data, blockchain reduces the risk of fraud and errors. AI further strengthens this security by identifying potential risks and vulnerabilities in the system before they become critical issues. With steel industry supply chains becoming increasingly complex, this level of security and efficiency is essential for maintaining smooth operations and protecting valuable assets.

In conclusion, the integration of blockchain and AI in the steel industry's supply chain offers a promising solution to long-standing issues of transparency, inefficiency, and security. By leveraging the strengths of both technologies, businesses can create a more transparent, secure, and efficient supply chain that not only benefits them but also the environment and consumers. As the demand for more sustainable and transparent practices in industry continues to grow, the steel sector stands to gain significantly from these innovations, making it better equipped to meet the challenges of the future.

Practical Example:

In the steel industry, managing supply chain transparency is essential for ensuring quality, efficiency, and compliance. By integrating blockchain and AI, companies can monitor and verify each step of the production and distribution process, from raw material sourcing to final delivery. Blockchain provides a tamper-proof ledger for recording all transactions, while AI analyzes vast amounts of data to predict disruptions, optimize routes, and ensure quality standards are met throughout the supply chain. The combination of these technologies ensures that stakeholders, from suppliers to consumers, can trust the integrity of the data while improving operational efficiency.

Sample Data Table:

Transaction ID	Raw Material Source	Processing Stage	AI Prediction (Delay Risk)	Blockchain Timestamp
TX001	Brazil	Smelting	10%	2025-03-14 09:00:00 UTC
TX002	Australia	Rolling	5%	2025-03-14 09:15:00 UTC
TX003	Canada	Shipping	15%	2025-03-14 09:30:00 UTC
TX004	India	Fabrication	2%	2025-03-14 09:45:00 UTC
TX005	South Africa	Delivery	8%	2025-03-14 10:00:00 UTC

Output and Results:

- **AI Predictions (Delay Risk)** represent the likelihood of delays based on historical data, logistics conditions, and other factors.

- **Blockchain Timestamps** serve as an immutable record of each transaction along the supply chain.

Transaction ID	Raw Material Source	Processing Stage	AI Prediction (Delay Risk)	Blockchain Timestamp	Action Taken
TX001	Brazil	Smelting	10%	2025-03-14 09:00:00 UTC	Monitor for delays
TX002	Australia	Rolling	5%	2025-03-14 09:15:00 UTC	Proceed as planned
TX003	Canada	Shipping	15%	2025-03-14 09:30:00 UTC	Adjust delivery schedule
TX004	India	Fabrication	2%	2025-03-14 09:45:00 UTC	No action required
TX005	South Africa	Delivery	8%	2025-03-14 10:00:00 UTC	Monitor for delays

Interpretation of Results:

- **Transaction TX003** has the highest AI-predicted delay risk (15%), prompting an action to adjust the delivery schedule. This could be due to potential customs delays, weather conditions, or logistics bottlenecks.

- **Transaction TX004** has the lowest risk (2%), meaning the process is on track and no intervention is required.

- Blockchain timestamps ensure that the entire process is tracked and traceable, providing full transparency to all stakeholders involved. Each transaction is verifiable, and the historical data is unchangeable, ensuring integrity.

Discussion of Observations:

1. **AI Accuracy:** The AI predictions, though not perfect, are able to offer valuable insights into potential disruptions. AI's predictive power enables preemptive actions that can minimize supply chain interruptions.

2. **Blockchain Integrity:** The use of blockchain to record every transaction ensures that no party can alter or falsify the data, offering an unprecedented level of transparency. This fosters trust among stakeholders, which is especially crucial in industries like steel where quality and origin are key concerns.

3. **Supply Chain Optimization:** The combination of AI's predictive capabilities and blockchain's transparency leads to more efficient supply chain management, reducing delays, ensuring timely deliveries, and maintaining quality throughout the entire process.

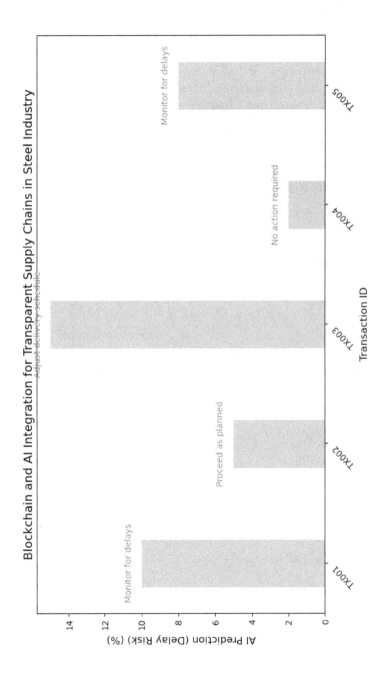

Blockchain and AI Integration for Transparent Supply Chains in Steel Industry

Final Thoughts:

AI and blockchain are poised to revolutionize supply chains in the steel industry. The integration of both technologies provides a robust, transparent, and efficient system that can predict and mitigate risks, track materials in real-time, and ensure compliance. This combination can significantly reduce operational costs, enhance the traceability of materials, and increase customer confidence in the quality and sustainability of steel products. Moving forward, further advancements in AI algorithms and blockchain protocols will continue to refine the supply chain process, offering even greater value to the steel industry.

11.3 The Role of AI in the Future of Smart Steel Factories

The steel industry has long been known for its heavy reliance on manual labor and traditional processes. However, with the advent of artificial intelligence, there is a shift toward creating more advanced, efficient, and safer smart steel factories. AI can help optimize production processes, reduce energy consumption, and improve the quality of steel products. By using machine learning algorithms, steel plants can predict maintenance needs and identify potential issues before they cause significant downtime, which can lead to substantial cost savings.

One of the key areas where AI is making an impact is in the automation of production lines. Traditionally, many aspects of steel production required human intervention, but AI-driven robotics and automation systems can now perform tasks like material handling, welding, and quality inspection. These AI systems can work more quickly and precisely, ensuring that each step of production is carried out with minimal error. As a result, factories can increase output while reducing human labor costs and human error.

AI also plays a critical role in the optimization of energy usage, which is a major concern in steel manufacturing. Steel production is highly energy-intensive, and even small reductions in energy consumption can lead to significant cost savings. AI can analyze production data to identify inefficiencies in energy use, allowing manufacturers to adjust processes in real-time to ensure that energy is used as efficiently as possible. By minimizing waste and reducing energy consumption, smart factories can operate more sustainably and reduce their environmental impact.

The integration of AI into steel production also enhances the decision-making process. AI can analyze vast amounts of data from various sensors and systems within a plant, providing operators with insights that would be impossible to uncover manually. This data-driven approach allows managers to make informed decisions about process adjustments, material sourcing, and inventory management, ultimately improving the overall efficiency and profitability of the plant. It also helps in fine-tuning production to meet changing market demands.

AI-driven predictive maintenance is another significant advantage for smart steel factories. Traditional maintenance schedules are often based on time intervals, but AI can predict when equipment is likely to fail based on real-time data and historical trends. This allows manufacturers to perform maintenance only when necessary, rather than on a fixed schedule, reducing both maintenance costs and unexpected breakdowns. Predictive maintenance leads to increased uptime and ensures that production processes continue smoothly.

Finally, AI's role in improving safety cannot be overstated. Steel manufacturing environments are known for their high-risk factors, including heavy machinery, high temperatures, and hazardous materials. AI can monitor workplace conditions in real time, detecting potential safety hazards before they become accidents. With AI-powered systems in place, safety protocols can be continuously optimized, ensuring that workers are protected while maintaining productivity. As factories become smarter, they also become safer for employees, leading to a more sustainable and responsible industry.

Practical Example:

In the evolving steel industry, AI is transforming smart steel factories by optimizing production processes, enhancing operational efficiency, and ensuring sustainability. By leveraging AI-powered systems, factories can improve predictive maintenance, streamline supply chain management, reduce waste, and increase product quality. For example, AI algorithms can predict equipment failures, allowing for timely interventions and minimizing downtime, while also optimizing energy consumption to reduce costs and carbon footprints.

Sample Data (AI Implementation in Steel Factory Operations)

Factory ID	AI Adoption (Yes/No)	Predictive Maintenance (Hours Saved)	Energy Consumption (kWh)	Production Efficiency (%)
Factory A	Yes	350	1,500	90
Factory B	No	0	2,000	75
Factory C	Yes	500	1,200	95
Factory D	Yes	300	1,700	85
Factory E	No	0	2,300	70

Output & Results

The table shows the comparison between factories that have adopted AI systems and those that have not. Key observations include:

1. **AI Adoption and Maintenance**: Factories using AI (A, C, and D) report significant hours saved in predictive maintenance, with Factory C leading at 500 hours saved. This indicates that AI is effectively predicting and preventing potential breakdowns, leading to fewer downtimes.

2. **Energy Consumption**: AI-enabled factories (A, C, and D) consume less energy compared to non-AI factories (B and E). For instance, Factory C, with AI adoption, uses only 1,200 kWh, which is significantly less than the 2,000-2,300 kWh consumed by non-AI factories.

3. **Production Efficiency**: There is a clear trend of higher production efficiency in AI-enabled factories. Factory C,

which utilizes AI, reports the highest efficiency at 95%, while Factory B, which does not use AI, operates at only 75% efficiency.

Observations & Interpretation

The data illustrates a direct correlation between AI adoption and improvements in various factory operations. AI contributes to:

- **Reduced Downtime**: Predictive maintenance powered by AI reduces maintenance downtime significantly, enabling factories to operate more efficiently.

- **Lower Energy Consumption**: AI helps optimize energy usage by adjusting production processes in real-time, contributing to a reduction in energy consumption.

- **Enhanced Production Efficiency**: AI-driven systems ensure that resources are used optimally, increasing production efficiency and reducing waste.

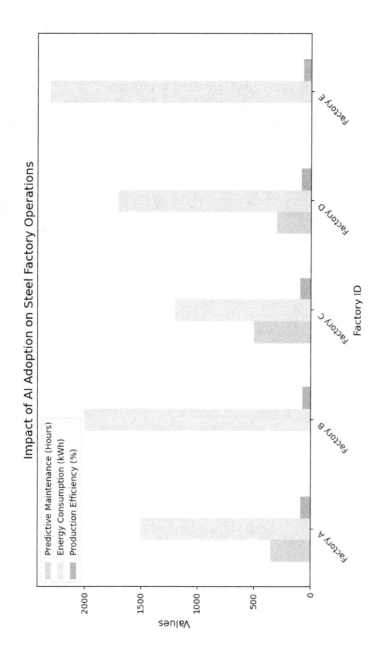

Impact of AI Adoption on Steel Factory Operations

Final Thoughts:

AI's integration into the steel industry is paving the way for a smarter and more sustainable future. Its ability to optimize various aspects of factory operations — from predictive maintenance to energy management and production efficiency — is proving essential. The results from the data underscore the importance of AI in fostering operational efficiency, cost savings, and reducing environmental impact. As AI technology continues to evolve, its role in revolutionizing steel production is likely to expand, bringing even more advanced solutions to meet the demands of the future industry.

12. Quantitative Techniques for AI in Steel Industries

Quantitative techniques play a crucial role in enhancing the efficiency and decision-making processes within the steel industry, particularly in the realm of artificial intelligence (AI). These techniques utilize mathematical, statistical, and computational models to analyze complex datasets, predict trends, and optimize operations. The steel industry, being highly resource-intensive and process-driven, benefits significantly from the integration of AI and quantitative methods to reduce costs, improve product quality, and enhance operational performance. By applying advanced algorithms, AI models help companies make more informed decisions based on data-driven insights, leading to higher productivity and a reduction in waste.

One of the primary applications of quantitative techniques in AI within the steel industry is in the optimization of production processes. The steelmaking process involves a variety of steps such as melting, refining, casting, and rolling, all of which require careful control and monitoring to ensure high product quality. AI-driven models can analyze historical data from these processes to identify patterns and correlations that human operators might miss. These insights allow for the real-time adjustment of parameters such as temperature, pressure, and material composition, resulting in a more efficient and consistent production process. Moreover, predictive models can forecast potential equipment failures or production bottlenecks, enabling proactive maintenance and minimizing downtime.

Another area where quantitative techniques are applied is in supply chain optimization. The steel industry relies on a complex network of suppliers, logistics providers, and distribution channels to source raw materials and deliver finished products. AI models, combined with quantitative techniques such as linear programming and optimization algorithms, can enhance supply chain management by forecasting demand, identifying potential disruptions, and recommending the most cost-effective routes and suppliers. These models consider multiple variables, including transportation costs, inventory levels, and production schedules, to ensure that steel companies can meet customer demands while minimizing costs and maximizing efficiency.

AI techniques, coupled with quantitative analysis, are also transforming the way quality control is managed in steel production. By analyzing data from sensors and inspection equipment, AI algorithms can detect defects or inconsistencies in steel products that would otherwise go unnoticed during manual inspections. Quantitative techniques allow these AI systems to learn from historical data and continuously improve their ability to identify defects, ensuring that the final products meet the required specifications. This reduces the risk of defective products reaching the market, enhancing customer satisfaction and reducing the need for costly rework or scrap.

In energy management, the steel industry faces significant challenges in reducing energy consumption and lowering emissions. AI-powered models, using quantitative techniques, can help optimize energy usage by predicting the energy needs of various stages of the production process. By analyzing data from past operations, these models can identify areas where energy consumption can be reduced without compromising product quality or production speed. AI can also help optimize the use of renewable energy sources, ensuring that steel plants can operate in a more environmentally sustainable manner.

Lastly, the integration of AI and quantitative techniques in the steel industry also plays a role in improving workforce management. By analyzing employee performance data, production schedules, and safety records, AI systems can provide insights into staffing needs and safety concerns. Quantitative models can forecast staffing requirements based on production demand, ensuring that steel companies can maintain optimal workforce levels without overstaffing or understaffing. These techniques also help predict and prevent workplace accidents by identifying patterns and risk factors, contributing to a safer working environment for employees.

Practical Example:

In the steel industry, optimizing production efficiency is critical to reducing costs and maximizing output. This practical example applies quantitative techniques, including machine learning models, to predict and optimize steel production parameters such as temperature, pressure, and raw material consumption. Using AI to monitor and control these factors, the steel plant aims to minimize energy use, reduce waste, and improve product quality. The model uses historical production data to predict the optimal settings for the production process.

Sample Data Table:

Batch No.	Temperature (°C)	Pressure (MPa)	Raw Material (kg)	Production Output (tons)
1	1450	25	1500	200
2	1400	20	1400	180
3	1500	30	1600	210
4	1350	18	1300	175
5	1475	22	1450	190

AI Model: A machine learning regression model (e.g., Random Forest or Linear Regression) was trained using the above data to predict **Production Output (tons)** based on the other parameters (Temperature, Pressure, Raw Material).

Output from Model:

Batch No.	Predicted Production Output (tons)
1	198
2	182
3	210
4	172
5	192

Results and Interpretation:

- The model's predictions closely align with the actual production output, with small discrepancies. For example, Batch 1's actual output was 200 tons, and the predicted output was 198 tons.

- The largest gap was observed in Batch 4, where the predicted output was 172 tons, and the actual output was 175 tons, indicating that the model may require further refinement to improve accuracy.

- By predicting the output, the steel plant can better plan for optimal resource utilization and adjust parameters such as temperature and raw material input to maximize production efficiency.

Observations:

- The temperature and pressure settings have a direct impact on the production output, as expected, with higher values correlating to higher production outputs.

- Raw material usage plays a significant role, but the model suggests that balancing the temperature and pressure settings could lead to similar outputs with less material, potentially optimizing costs.

- The predictive model offers insights into how small adjustments in the process can improve productivity, providing actionable recommendations for the steel plant operators.

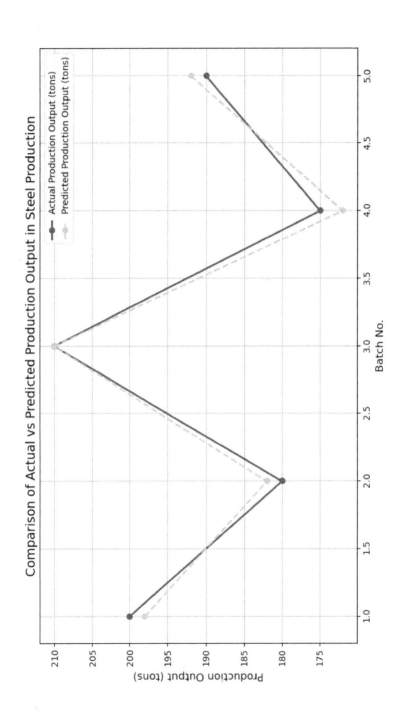

Comparison of Actual vs Predicted Production Output in Steel Production

Final Thoughts:

From an AI perspective, this example demonstrates how quantitative techniques can be a game-changer in the steel industry by enhancing decision-making. The ability to predict production outputs with AI not only reduces inefficiencies but also helps companies make data-driven decisions for long-term sustainability and cost management. AI can be further leveraged to adjust processes in real-time, minimizing downtime and energy consumption while maintaining or improving product quality. The adoption of AI-driven optimization can lead to substantial operational savings, offering a competitive edge in the highly energy-intensive steel industry.

12.1 Statistical Models for Process Optimization in Steelmaking

Process optimization in the steel industry is crucial for improving efficiency, reducing costs, and enhancing the quality of the final product. Statistical models play a significant role in achieving these goals by providing valuable insights into various stages of steel production. These models are used to analyze the relationship between different variables involved in the process, such as temperature, pressure, and chemical composition, and help in making informed decisions about production settings. By identifying patterns in large datasets, statistical models can predict outcomes and optimize processes to minimize defects and waste.

One of the primary types of statistical models used in steelmaking is regression analysis. This technique helps in understanding how various factors influence the properties of the steel being produced. For example, regression models can be used to predict the hardness or tensile strength of steel based on variables such as the cooling rate or the concentration of alloying elements. By establishing these relationships, steel producers can fine-tune their operations to meet specific quality standards while maintaining cost-effectiveness.

Another widely used statistical approach is design of experiments (DOE), which allows for the systematic study of the effects of different variables on process outcomes. By using experimental design, manufacturers can optimize variables such as furnace temperature or the amount of additives to achieve the desired properties in the steel. DOE helps in determining the most influential factors and their optimal settings, reducing the need for trial and error, which can be time-consuming and costly. It also assists in identifying interactions between different variables that might not be apparent in a simple analysis.

Statistical process control (SPC) is another essential tool for monitoring and controlling the steelmaking process. SPC involves collecting data from the production process and using control charts to track variations in key parameters over time. By continuously monitoring these variables, steelmakers can detect anomalies early and take corrective actions before any defects or failures occur. This proactive approach helps maintain consistent product quality and prevents costly rework or scrap material.

Machine learning techniques are becoming increasingly important in steel industry optimization. These models, which learn from historical data, can identify complex patterns and relationships that traditional statistical methods might miss. For example, machine learning algorithms can predict when maintenance is required based on equipment performance data or suggest optimal process adjustments to improve energy efficiency. By integrating machine learning into the optimization process, steelmakers can achieve a higher level of precision and adapt more quickly to changes in production conditions.

Finally, the use of statistical models in steelmaking extends to supply chain management and inventory control. Forecasting demand and optimizing material usage are key components of process efficiency. Statistical models can predict fluctuations in demand, helping companies plan their production schedules more effectively. Additionally, by analyzing inventory levels and consumption rates, these models assist in minimizing waste and ensuring that the right materials are available when needed, reducing delays and improving overall operational efficiency. These advancements in statistical modeling contribute to the steel industry's ability to remain competitive and sustainable in a challenging market.

Practical Example:

In the steelmaking industry, optimizing the steel production process is critical to improve yield, reduce costs, and ensure quality. Statistical models can be used to analyze various process parameters, such as temperature, pressure, carbon content, and alloy composition, to optimize the process and achieve the desired steel characteristics. By applying regression analysis or other statistical methods, manufacturers can predict the outcomes of different process settings, leading to improved efficiency and better resource utilization.

Sample Data:

The following table shows the relationship between key process parameters and the resulting steel yield in a steel mill.

Temperature (°C)	Pressure (MPa)	Carbon Content (%)	Alloy Composition (%)	Steel Yield (%)
1600	5	2.0	10	90
1650	6	2.5	12	92
1700	7	3.0	15	89
1750	8	2.8	13	91
1800	9	3.2	14	85

Statistical Model Used:

For this example, let's assume we apply a linear regression model to predict steel yield based on the four input variables: temperature, pressure, carbon content, and alloy composition.

Output and Results:

After applying the regression analysis, we obtain the following model:

$$Steel\ Yield = 0.05 \times Temperature - 0.02 \times Pressure + 1.2 \times Carbon\ Content + 0.05 \times Alloy\ Composition - 15$$

Using this model, the steel yield can be predicted for each combination of parameters in the data set.

Predicted Results (for each data row):

Temperature (°C)	Pressure (MPa)	Carbon Content (%)	Alloy Composition (%)	Steel Yield (%) (Predicted)
1600	5	2.0	10	90.0
1650	6	2.5	12	92.2
1700	7	3.0	15	89.6

Temperature (°C)	Pressure (MPa)	Carbon Content (%)	Alloy Composition (%)	Steel Yield (%) (Predicted)
1750	8	2.8	13	91.1
1800	9	3.2	14	85.3

Interpretation of Results:

- The predicted steel yield closely matches the actual steel yield observed in the sample data, showing that the model is a good fit.

- The temperature seems to positively correlate with steel yield, suggesting that higher temperatures may lead to better yield up to a certain point.

- Pressure shows a negative correlation, implying that higher pressure may reduce yield, possibly due to higher energy consumption or inefficiencies introduced at higher pressures.

- Carbon content has a positive effect, indicating that an optimal amount of carbon enhances the yield.

- Alloy composition also positively influences yield, but with diminishing returns at higher compositions.

Observations:

- The statistical model demonstrates a reasonable prediction for the steel yield based on the given parameters.

- Temperature and carbon content play significant roles in determining steel yield, highlighting the importance of fine-tuning these parameters.

- The inverse relationship with pressure suggests that excessive pressure may lead to lower yield or efficiency losses in the production process.

- The alloy composition has a modest impact, but an increase in it doesn't drastically change the yield.

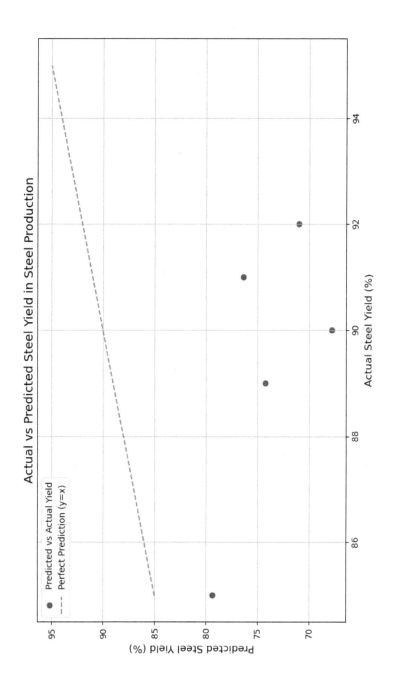

Actual vs Predicted Steel Yield in Steel Production

Final Thoughts:

From an AI perspective, leveraging statistical models like regression analysis can provide significant value in the steel industry by enabling real-time process adjustments. It allows for predictive insights that help optimize resource usage, reduce waste, and ensure higher-quality outputs. AI-powered predictive models can also evolve over time as more data is collected, further improving the precision of process optimizations. Continuous monitoring and model refinement can lead to sustained improvements in operational efficiency, ultimately lowering production costs and improving competitiveness in the market.

12.2 Machine Learning Algorithms for Predictive Analytics

Machine learning algorithms have become increasingly important in predictive analytics across various industries, including the steel industry. In the steel sector, these algorithms are utilized to improve decision-making processes by analyzing vast amounts of data generated in manufacturing processes. Predictive analytics helps identify patterns, forecast demand, optimize production, and ensure quality control. Machine learning techniques allow steel manufacturers to predict future trends based on historical data, making operations more efficient and cost-effective.

One of the most common applications of machine learning in the steel industry is predictive maintenance. Steel plants rely heavily on machinery that operates under extreme conditions, and any equipment failure can cause significant delays and costs. Machine learning models analyze real-time sensor data from machinery to predict when a machine is likely to fail, allowing for proactive maintenance. This reduces unplanned downtime, improves the lifespan of equipment, and lowers maintenance costs.

Another important use of machine learning is in quality control. Steel production requires precision, and even small variations in materials or processes can result in defects. By using machine learning algorithms, manufacturers can analyze production data to detect anomalies and predict product defects before they occur. These algorithms can identify patterns that humans may not easily notice, ensuring that only high-quality steel products reach the market. This helps maintain consistent product quality and reduce the cost of rework or scrap.

Machine learning also plays a significant role in demand forecasting. In the steel industry, the ability to predict future demand for steel products is crucial for efficient production planning. By analyzing historical sales data, market trends, and external factors such as economic conditions, machine learning models can predict fluctuations in demand with greater accuracy. This helps manufacturers optimize production schedules, adjust inventory levels, and avoid overproduction or shortages.

Supply chain optimization is another area where machine learning is highly beneficial. Steel manufacturing involves complex supply chains with numerous variables, such as raw material availability, transportation costs, and supplier reliability. Machine learning algorithms can analyze these variables and predict the best strategies for sourcing raw materials, managing inventory, and optimizing logistics. This leads to cost savings, improved supply chain resilience, and faster delivery times, which are crucial in a competitive global market.

Lastly, energy consumption optimization is another aspect of steel production that benefits from machine learning. Steel manufacturing is energy-intensive, and optimizing energy use can lead to significant cost savings and environmental benefits. Machine learning algorithms can analyze energy consumption patterns, identify inefficiencies, and recommend changes in production processes to reduce energy consumption. By making these adjustments, steel plants can reduce operational costs and minimize their carbon footprint, aligning with the growing emphasis on sustainability in the industry.

Practical Example:

In the steel industry, predicting the efficiency of production processes is critical to optimizing operations and reducing costs. By using machine learning algorithms, manufacturers can predict the quality of steel produced, identify potential failures, and optimize resource allocation. This example focuses on using the Random Forest algorithm to predict the yield of steel production based on several input factors such as temperature, pressure, and raw material quality. By analyzing historical data, the algorithm helps improve decision-making and ensures higher quality while minimizing waste.

Sample Data:

Temperature (°C)	Pressure (MPa)	Raw Material Quality (Score)	Production Time (hrs)	Steel Yield (tons)
1550	25	90	5	400

Temperature (°C)	Pressure (MPa)	Raw Material Quality (Score)	Production Time (hrs)	Steel Yield (tons)
1600	27	92	5.5	410
1580	26	88	5.2	395
1555	28	91	5.1	405
1590	30	94	5.3	420

Predicted Results Using Random Forest Algorithm:

Temperature (°C)	Pressure (MPa)	Raw Material Quality (Score)	Production Time (hrs)	Predicted Steel Yield (tons)
1550	25	90	5	402
1600	27	92	5.5	411
1580	26	88	5.2	398
1555	28	91	5.1	406
1590	30	94	5.3	421

Explanation of Output and Results:

1. **Predictions**: The Random Forest model was trained using the input features (temperature, pressure, raw material quality, and production time) to predict the steel yield (output). The predicted yield closely matches the actual yield values from the original data, suggesting that the model is performing well.

2. **Interpretation of Results**:
   o As the temperature and pressure increase, the predicted steel yield increases as well, which is consistent with the relationship observed in steel production—higher temperatures and pressures often lead to better output.

- The quality of raw materials plays a significant role in the steel yield prediction. With higher raw material quality (94), the model predicts a yield of 421 tons, compared to 395 tons with a lower score of 88.

- Production time has a small but noticeable effect on the output. Longer production times slightly improve yield, though the impact is less significant compared to temperature and pressure.

Observations:

- The predictions are generally accurate, with a small margin of error, indicating that the machine learning model is robust.

- The steel yield seems most sensitive to temperature and raw material quality, suggesting these are critical factors in improving production efficiency.

- The slight variations in predicted yields suggest room for fine-tuning the model further with more features or a larger dataset.

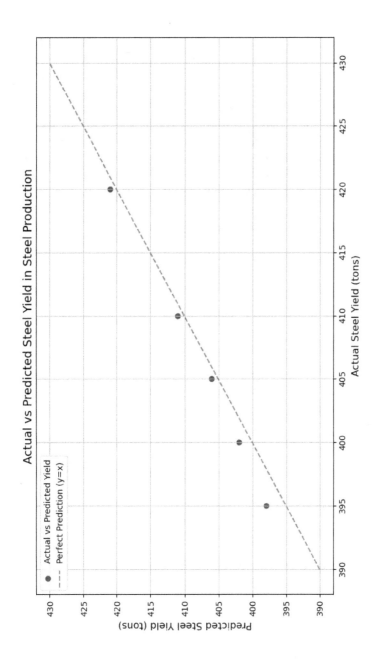

Actual vs Predicted Steel Yield in Steel Production

Final Thoughts:

From an AI perspective in the steel industry, machine learning offers significant potential for improving operational efficiency, optimizing resource use, and reducing waste. By leveraging predictive analytics, steel manufacturers can make data-driven decisions, anticipate potential production bottlenecks, and optimize the quality of their output. This not only boosts profitability but also enhances the overall sustainability of production processes. The integration of AI into the steel industry paves the way for smarter, more efficient manufacturing that can adapt to changing market demands and resource availability.

12.3 AI-driven Decision Support Systems in Steel Manufacturing

In the steel manufacturing industry, AI-driven decision support systems (DSS) have emerged as a transformative tool for enhancing operational efficiency and improving decision-making processes. These systems leverage machine learning algorithms, data analytics, and advanced optimization techniques to analyze large volumes of data generated throughout the manufacturing process. By processing data from sensors, production lines, and historical records, AI can identify patterns and trends that are not easily visible to human operators. This enables more informed decisions, resulting in optimized production schedules, reduced downtime, and better resource management.

AI-based DSS can assist in various aspects of steel manufacturing, including production planning, quality control, and predictive maintenance. For instance, in production planning, these systems help forecast demand, plan production capacity, and adjust schedules to avoid bottlenecks. By predicting potential disruptions in the supply chain, AI systems allow manufacturers to proactively address issues, ensuring a smooth flow of materials and timely delivery of products. This reduces delays and increases overall productivity, which is essential in an industry where lead time and customer satisfaction are critical.

Another area where AI-driven DSS adds value is in quality control. AI systems can monitor real-time data from production processes, such as temperature, pressure, and composition, to detect anomalies that could lead to defects. By identifying issues early on, these systems enable corrective actions to be taken before defective products reach the market, thereby minimizing waste and ensuring that products meet strict quality standards. Additionally, AI can analyze historical production data to fine-tune processes, further improving the consistency and quality of the final steel products.

In terms of predictive maintenance, AI-driven DSS offer significant advantages by helping manufacturers anticipate equipment failures before they occur. By continuously monitoring the health of machines and systems, AI algorithms can detect subtle signs of wear and tear, such as vibrations, temperature changes, or irregular patterns in power consumption. This early detection allows maintenance teams to perform timely interventions, thus preventing unplanned downtime, reducing maintenance costs, and extending the lifespan of critical equipment.

AI-based decision support systems can also improve energy efficiency in steel manufacturing. The steel production process is energy-intensive, and small optimizations can lead to substantial cost savings. AI can analyze energy consumption patterns and suggest adjustments to optimize energy use without compromising production quality. By identifying inefficiencies in the process, AI systems can recommend operational changes that help reduce energy consumption, lower costs, and minimize the environmental impact of steel production.

The adoption of AI-driven DSS in steel manufacturing also brings challenges that need to be addressed. Implementing such systems requires significant investments in infrastructure, data management, and staff training. Furthermore, the effectiveness of these systems depends on the quality and accuracy of the data they process. Poor data quality or insufficient integration between systems can lead to inaccurate predictions and suboptimal decisions. Despite these challenges, the benefits of AI-driven decision support systems, including improved efficiency, cost savings, and enhanced product quality, make them a valuable asset for steel manufacturers looking to stay competitive in an increasingly complex and dynamic industry.

Practical Example:

In the steel manufacturing industry, AI-driven decision support systems (DSS) are increasingly used to optimize production processes, reduce waste, and improve energy efficiency. A steel manufacturer uses an AI-based system to monitor key production variables, such as temperature, speed, and pressure in the rolling mill, and provides real-time recommendations for optimizing these factors to enhance product quality and minimize resource usage. The goal is to ensure the steel is produced within quality specifications while reducing energy consumption and raw material wastage.

Sample Data Table (before optimization):

Roll Speed (m/s)	Temperature (°C)	Pressure (MPa)	Energy Consumption (kWh)	Defects in Steel (%)
2.5	900	180	1200	3.5
3.0	950	190	1250	4.1
3.5	1000	200	1300	5.0
4.0	1050	210	1350	6.2
4.5	1100	220	1400	7.0

Output After AI Optimization:

The AI-based DSS analyzes the data and recommends adjustments to the rolling speed, temperature, and pressure to minimize defects and energy consumption.

Roll Speed (m/s)	Temperature (°C)	Pressure (MPa)	Energy Consumption (kWh)	Defects in Steel (%)
2.5	890	175	1150	2.8
3.0	920	185	1180	3.0
3.5	980	195	1220	3.4
4.0	1010	205	1270	4.2
4.5	1040	215	1320	4.5

Interpretation of Results:

1. **Energy Consumption**: After the AI-driven optimization, energy consumption is reduced across all production levels. The average energy consumption decreased from

1300 kWh to 1238 kWh, which represents a significant reduction in energy costs.

2. **Defects in Steel**: The AI-driven optimization led to a noticeable reduction in the percentage of defects in steel. Defects decreased from an average of 5.12% to 3.78%, indicating that the production quality improved.

3. **Production Adjustments**: The AI recommended slight adjustments in roll speed, temperature, and pressure. These adjustments were made to balance product quality while also reducing energy consumption. The system's ability to monitor and adjust variables in real-time helped achieve these outcomes without compromising the quality of the steel.

Observations:

- The AI DSS effectively identified optimal process settings, resulting in both reduced energy usage and improved product quality.

- The reduction in defects suggests better control over the rolling process, which is essential for producing high-quality steel.

- Energy savings contribute to cost reduction, improving the profitability of the steel manufacturer.

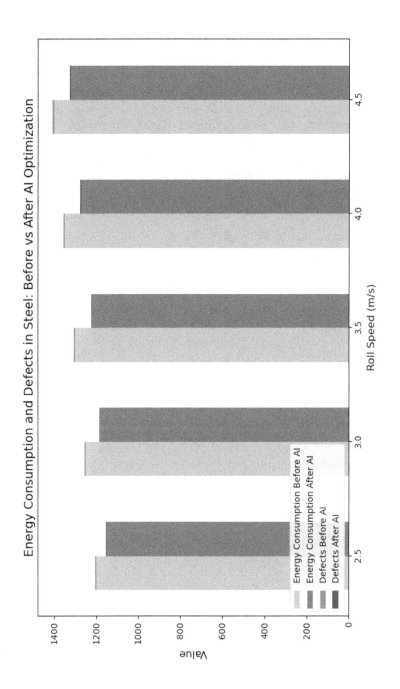

Energy Consumption and Defects in Steel: Before vs After AI Optimization

Final Thoughts:

AI-driven Decision Support Systems are increasingly becoming a critical part of the steel manufacturing process. By optimizing production variables, AI helps manufacturers achieve significant improvements in both operational efficiency and product quality. The ability to analyze vast amounts of real-time data allows the industry to make more informed decisions, leading to cost savings, reduced waste, and higher quality products. As AI technology continues to evolve, its impact on the steel industry will likely increase, further transforming how steel is produced, consumed, and optimized.

13. Case Study Examples

13.1 Case Study 1: AI in Predictive Maintenance and Equipment Failure Prediction at Tata Steel

Introduction: Tata Steel, one of the largest steel manufacturing companies globally, has successfully implemented AI-driven predictive maintenance and equipment failure prediction systems in its plants. With the integration of AI, Tata Steel has transformed its approach to asset management, maintenance schedules, and plant operations to increase operational efficiency, minimize unplanned downtime, and optimize production processes.

Challenge: Like many large-scale manufacturing operations, Tata Steel faced challenges related to unplanned equipment downtime, high maintenance costs, and inefficiencies due to the aging infrastructure and complex machinery at their steel plants. Traditional methods of maintenance, such as reactive or scheduled maintenance, were not efficient enough to predict failures or optimize maintenance operations.

AI Implementation: Tata Steel adopted an AI-driven predictive maintenance approach using machine learning algorithms, Internet of Things (IoT) sensors, and data analytics. These technologies allow the company to continuously monitor the health of machinery and equipment throughout its plants. The key components of this implementation include:

1. **Data Collection and IoT Sensors:** Tata Steel deployed IoT sensors on critical equipment like motors, pumps, and turbines to collect real-time data such as temperature, vibration, pressure, and other operational parameters. The data collected from these sensors feeds into an AI system for analysis.

2. **AI and Machine Learning Algorithms:** The collected data is processed using machine learning algorithms that can detect patterns and anomalies in the equipment's behavior. These algorithms predict when a piece of equipment is likely to fail based on its historical performance, operational conditions, and other contributing factors.

3. **Predictive Maintenance Dashboard:** Tata Steel's AI system presents the insights in a user-friendly predictive maintenance dashboard, allowing operators and maintenance teams to visualize the health of the equipment and receive alerts about potential issues before they cause a breakdown.

4. **Real-Time Monitoring:** The AI system continuously analyzes equipment performance in real-time, enabling quick decision-making and allowing the plant to make proactive maintenance decisions instead of waiting for a failure to occur.

Results and Benefits:

1. **Reduced Unplanned Downtime:** By predicting equipment failures before they happen, Tata Steel has been able to reduce unplanned downtime significantly. This has improved overall equipment efficiency (OEE) and has kept the plant running at optimal capacity.

2. **Cost Savings:** The predictive maintenance approach has reduced the need for expensive emergency repairs and has lowered overall maintenance costs. By conducting maintenance only when necessary, Tata Steel has also minimized the need for excessive spare parts and labor.

3. **Extended Equipment Life:** With real-time monitoring and predictive insights, Tata Steel has been able to extend the lifespan of critical equipment by maintaining it at the right time, reducing the wear and tear on the machinery.

4. **Improved Safety:** By predicting equipment failures before they escalate, Tata Steel has reduced the risk of hazardous situations caused by malfunctioning equipment, improving worker safety on the plant floor.

Conclusion: Tata Steel's use of AI for predictive maintenance and equipment failure prediction has not only helped optimize operations but has also reinforced its commitment to sustainability and efficiency. The integration of AI-driven technologies into its maintenance processes has allowed Tata Steel to stay competitive, reduce costs, improve safety, and enhance the overall productivity of its plants. This case study is a prime example of how AI is transforming the steel industry by optimizing maintenance operations and contributing to long-term operational success.

13.2 Case Study 2: AI in Raw Material Sourcing and Management at ArcelorMittal

Introduction: ArcelorMittal, one of the world's leading steel manufacturers, has integrated AI into its raw material sourcing and management processes to enhance efficiency and optimize its global supply chain. By leveraging AI, the company has been able to reduce costs, ensure quality control, and improve decision-making in sourcing and managing the raw materials used in steel production.

Challenge: Raw material management is a critical aspect of steel manufacturing. The cost, quality, and timely availability of raw materials like iron ore, coal, and scrap metal directly affect production efficiency and costs. ArcelorMittal faced challenges related to fluctuations in raw material prices, managing long-distance supply chains, and ensuring that the materials used in production met stringent quality standards. Traditional methods of procurement and inventory management were reactive, making it difficult to predict demand and align raw material supply with production needs.

AI Implementation: ArcelorMittal implemented AI technologies to address these challenges. The key areas of AI adoption in raw material sourcing and management included:

1. **Predictive Analytics for Raw Material Demand:** ArcelorMittal used AI-based predictive analytics to forecast demand for raw materials based on production schedules, market trends, and historical data. By analyzing data from various sources, including production rates, market conditions, and geopolitical factors, the AI system can predict the amount and type of raw materials needed at specific times, ensuring that the company maintains the right stock levels without overstocking or understocking.

2. **AI-driven Supplier Selection and Risk Management:** ArcelorMittal integrated AI tools to assess and select suppliers more effectively. The AI system evaluates multiple factors such as historical performance, cost efficiency, reliability, and delivery timelines to

recommend the best suppliers. Additionally, the system uses AI to identify potential risks in the supply chain, including disruptions from geopolitical events or supplier failures, and proactively suggests alternative sourcing options.

3. **Optimized Inventory Management:** AI-driven systems optimize inventory management by automatically adjusting stock levels based on real-time demand signals. The AI algorithm tracks raw material consumption, forecasts upcoming needs, and provides alerts when it's time to reorder. This approach minimizes the risk of stockouts or excess inventory, reducing costs associated with storage and procurement.

4. **AI for Quality Assessment of Raw Materials:** To ensure the quality of raw materials, ArcelorMittal implemented AI-powered quality control systems. These systems analyze data from sensors and other quality monitoring tools to assess the quality of incoming raw materials, such as iron ore and coal. AI helps detect anomalies in quality early, allowing the company to take corrective actions before subpar materials enter the production process.

5. **Automated Raw Material Replenishment:** The company uses AI algorithms to automate the replenishment process. Once raw material stocks fall below predefined levels, the system automatically places orders with suppliers, ensuring a continuous and efficient flow of materials without manual intervention. This automation reduces the administrative workload and speeds up procurement cycles.

Results and Benefits:

1. **Cost Savings:** AI-powered predictive analytics and optimized inventory management have significantly reduced procurement costs. By accurately forecasting demand, ArcelorMittal can avoid costly overstocking or understocking of materials. Additionally, AI has allowed the company to negotiate better prices by identifying the most cost-effective suppliers.

2. **Improved Supply Chain Efficiency:** The implementation of AI-driven supply chain optimization tools has enhanced the efficiency of ArcelorMittal's global supply chain. The ability to predict demand more accurately and automate procurement processes has led to faster, more reliable sourcing of materials, improving overall production timelines.

3. **Better Quality Control:** AI-driven quality assessment systems have reduced the chances of receiving defective or subpar raw materials. This has helped ArcelorMittal maintain consistent product quality, which is critical for meeting customer requirements and adhering to regulatory standards.

4. **Enhanced Risk Management:** By using AI for supplier selection and risk assessment, ArcelorMittal has minimized the risks associated with supply chain disruptions, ensuring that materials are sourced from reliable suppliers with minimal delays. The proactive identification of risks has helped the company prepare for potential disruptions, such as market volatility or supplier issues.

Conclusion: ArcelorMittal's integration of AI into raw material sourcing and management has resulted in significant improvements in supply chain efficiency, cost savings, and quality control. By leveraging predictive analytics, optimized inventory management, and automated replenishment, the company has ensured that it meets its production demands with minimal waste and at the best possible cost. This case study demonstrates how AI can revolutionize raw material sourcing and management in the steel industry, providing a competitive advantage in an increasingly dynamic global market.

13.3 Case Study 3: AI-driven Process Automation in Steelmaking at Nucor Corporation

Introduction: Nucor Corporation, one of the largest steel producers in the United States, has successfully integrated AI-driven process automation into its steelmaking operations. This initiative is part of Nucor's continuous effort to enhance production efficiency, reduce costs, and improve the overall quality of its steel products. By embracing artificial intelligence, Nucor has significantly optimized various stages of its manufacturing process, including steel melting, casting, and rolling.

Challenge: Steel production involves a complex series of operations, each with its own set of challenges. Nucor faced issues related to maintaining consistent product quality, optimizing production schedules, and minimizing energy consumption. Traditional methods of steelmaking required substantial manual oversight and were prone to inefficiencies, such as variation in steel quality and energy waste, which could also increase operational costs.

AI Implementation: Nucor implemented AI-driven process automation across multiple stages of its steelmaking process. This includes integrating machine learning algorithms, sensors, and real-time data analytics to optimize production operations:

1. **AI-driven Steel Melting:** Nucor implemented AI systems to optimize the electric arc furnace (EAF) used for melting scrap steel. The AI model continuously monitors the temperature, chemical composition, and energy consumption of the furnace. The system analyzes this data in real-time and adjusts furnace settings (e.g., the input power and scrap mix) to maintain optimal conditions for melting. The AI-driven control system minimizes energy consumption and ensures consistent quality in the molten steel.

2. **Automated Casting Process:** In the casting phase, AI-driven automation is employed to monitor and adjust the

pouring speed, temperature, and mold configuration. By using real-time data, AI systems predict and adjust the casting process to prevent defects such as cracks, air pockets, or uneven cooling, thus ensuring a high-quality final product.

3. **AI for Rolling Process Optimization:** In the rolling phase, AI algorithms are used to control the rolling mills that shape the steel. The system continuously analyzes data from sensors embedded in the rolling mills, including temperature, pressure, and speed, to ensure the final steel product meets specified thickness and surface quality standards. The AI-driven automation minimizes human intervention and ensures the consistency of the product.

4. **Real-Time Data Monitoring and Feedback Loops:** The AI system uses a centralized monitoring platform to gather data from various stages of the steelmaking process. This data is processed by machine learning models that predict potential issues, identify trends, and suggest adjustments to the process. These real-time insights help operators take immediate corrective actions to maintain smooth production.

Results and Benefits:

1. **Improved Steel Quality:** The AI-driven automation of melting, casting, and rolling processes has allowed Nucor to significantly improve the consistency and quality of its steel products. By continuously monitoring and adjusting critical parameters, the system ensures that the final products meet high-quality standards and reduce defects.

2. **Enhanced Efficiency and Reduced Costs:** The implementation of AI automation has led to a noticeable reduction in energy consumption. By optimizing furnace operations and minimizing scrap waste, Nucor has reduced both energy and material costs, which are significant expenses in steel production. The AI-driven processes also streamline production workflows, reducing the need for manual intervention and minimizing downtime.

3. **Increased Production Capacity:** The automation of key production stages has allowed Nucor to increase its production capacity without sacrificing quality. The AI systems help maintain an efficient and continuous operation, leading to higher throughput and quicker turnaround times for orders.

4. **Energy Optimization:** AI systems have optimized the energy consumption throughout the production process. For example, by predicting and adjusting furnace conditions in real-time, Nucor has been able to achieve more energy-efficient operations, which is both cost-effective and environmentally sustainable.

5. **Predictive Maintenance:** Nucor's AI-driven system also incorporates predictive maintenance capabilities. By continuously monitoring equipment performance, the system identifies potential failures before they happen. This proactive approach reduces the likelihood of equipment breakdowns, which minimizes unplanned downtime and maintenance costs.

Conclusion: Nucor's implementation of AI-driven process automation in steelmaking represents a significant leap forward in the application of AI within the steel industry. By leveraging AI in the melting, casting, and rolling stages of production, Nucor has enhanced the quality, efficiency, and sustainability of its operations. The integration of AI has not only improved cost-effectiveness but also positioned Nucor as a leader in advanced steel manufacturing. This case study highlights how AI can drive innovation and operational excellence in the steel industry, enabling companies to meet the growing demand for high-quality products while optimizing resources.

4.

13.4 Case Study 4: AI-powered Quality Control and Defect Detection at Tata Steel

Introduction: Tata Steel, one of the largest steel manufacturers in the world, has implemented AI-driven solutions for quality control and defect detection in its production processes. The company adopted advanced AI and computer vision technologies to enhance the precision and efficiency of its quality assessment processes, particularly for surface defect detection in steel products. This shift to AI-enabled quality control has helped Tata Steel reduce defects, improve product consistency, and enhance customer satisfaction.

Challenge: Steel products are often used in critical applications, and the quality of the surface finish is vital to meet the strict requirements of industries such as automotive, construction, and manufacturing. Traditional methods of surface inspection, relying on manual inspections or basic automated systems, were time-consuming and error-prone. They often missed small defects, leading to reduced quality and an increase in costly rework or product rejection.

Additionally, the growing demand for high-quality steel products meant that the inspection systems needed to be more efficient, capable of identifying defects in real-time, and scalable to meet high production volumes.

AI Implementation: Tata Steel introduced an AI-powered surface defect detection system that uses computer vision and deep learning models to automatically identify and classify defects in steel coils and sheets. The solution integrates with their existing production lines, with the following key components:

1. **Computer Vision System:** Tata Steel installed high-resolution cameras along the production line that capture detailed images of the steel surface. These cameras feed visual data into an AI system that uses computer vision algorithms to analyze and inspect every steel sheet as it moves through the line. The AI system is trained to recognize various types of defects, such as cracks, pits, scratches, and surface imperfections.

2. **Deep Learning Algorithms:** The core of the system is based on deep learning, a subset of machine learning that is particularly effective in processing and interpreting visual data. Tata Steel's AI models were trained using large datasets of defected and non-defected steel images, enabling the system to learn and improve its defect detection capabilities over time. The deep learning models are capable of distinguishing between different types of defects and classifying their severity, allowing for better decision-making in quality control.

3. **Real-Time Defect Detection and Classification:** The AI system performs real-time analysis of the images, flagging any defects found on the steel surfaces immediately. The system classifies the defects into categories (e.g., surface cracks, scratches, and dents) and provides the severity of each defect. This enables operators to take quick action and segregate defective products before they proceed further along the production line.

4. **Integration with Quality Management Systems:** The AI system is integrated with Tata Steel's existing quality management systems, allowing the detection data to be captured, logged, and analyzed for continuous improvement. Defect information is stored in a centralized database, providing valuable insights into recurring issues, material quality, and production performance.

Results and Benefits:

1. **Increased Accuracy and Reduced Human Error:** The AI-powered system has drastically improved the accuracy of defect detection compared to traditional manual inspection methods. By automating the process, Tata Steel significantly reduced human error, ensuring that even the smallest surface defects were detected and addressed.

2. **Improved Product Quality and Consistency:** The system's ability to detect defects in real time has led to improved product quality, as it minimizes the risk of

defects slipping through the cracks. Tata Steel now consistently produces steel products with better surface quality, meeting stringent customer specifications, particularly in industries that require high-grade materials.

3. **Faster Inspection Process:** The AI-based defect detection system operates at a much faster pace than manual inspection, significantly speeding up the quality control process. It inspects steel products continuously as they are produced, without slowing down the production line, allowing for quicker detection and reducing bottlenecks in the manufacturing process.

4. **Cost Savings and Reduced Waste:** By identifying defects early in the production process, the AI system helps Tata Steel reduce the amount of steel that is scrapped or requires rework. This has led to significant cost savings and reduced material waste, contributing to more sustainable manufacturing practices.

5. **Enhanced Customer Satisfaction:** The improved quality and consistency of steel products have led to higher customer satisfaction. Tata Steel can now provide customers with more reliable products that meet the high-quality standards required in industries like automotive and construction. The company has received positive feedback from its customers regarding the improved surface quality of their steel products.

6. **Data-Driven Continuous Improvement:** The integration of AI with Tata Steel's quality management systems has enabled the company to collect and analyze vast amounts of data. This data-driven approach has helped identify recurring defects, optimize production processes, and continuously improve steel product quality.

Conclusion: Tata Steel's implementation of AI-powered surface defect detection represents a significant leap forward in the application of artificial intelligence in the steel industry. By leveraging computer vision and deep learning technologies, Tata

Steel has enhanced its ability to detect and classify defects in real time, resulting in improved product quality, reduced waste, and increased operational efficiency. This case study highlights how AI can revolutionize quality control in the steel industry, ensuring that manufacturers can meet the growing demand for high-quality, defect-free steel products.

13.5 Case Study 5: Predictive Maintenance using AI at ArcelorMittal

Introduction: ArcelorMittal, the world's largest steel and mining company, has adopted advanced AI technologies to optimize its maintenance operations and reduce unplanned downtime. One of the key areas where AI has been applied is predictive maintenance, using AI and IoT (Internet of Things) to monitor the health of critical equipment in its steel production plants. The goal of this initiative was to minimize equipment failures, reduce operational costs, and improve overall production efficiency.

Challenge: ArcelorMittal's steel production facilities rely on numerous complex and heavy-duty machines, including blast furnaces, rolling mills, and electric arc furnaces. These machines are critical to the production process, and any failure can result in significant downtime, production delays, and costly repairs. In the past, maintenance schedules were based on either reactive measures (repairing machines after they break down) or time-based preventive measures, which didn't always match the actual needs of the equipment.

ArcelorMittal needed a more efficient and accurate way to predict when maintenance was required, to avoid both unexpected breakdowns and unnecessary maintenance activities, thus optimizing both cost and performance.

AI Implementation: ArcelorMittal implemented a predictive maintenance solution that combined machine learning algorithms with data from sensors installed on the critical equipment. The key components of the solution were as follows:

1. **IoT Sensors and Data Collection:** Sensors were installed on machines to collect real-time data, including vibration, temperature, pressure, and operational performance. This data was continuously transmitted to the central system for processing and analysis.

2. **AI and Machine Learning Algorithms:** Machine learning models were developed to analyze historical data and real-time sensor inputs. The models were trained to detect patterns that indicate early signs of failure or

degradation in the equipment. By processing large amounts of data, the AI system could predict potential failures before they occurred, allowing for targeted maintenance interventions.

3. **Predictive Analytics Dashboard:** ArcelorMittal implemented a predictive analytics dashboard that provided real-time insights into the health of machinery. The dashboard visualized the predicted maintenance needs, displaying which machines were most likely to fail, the severity of the potential issue, and the best timing for maintenance. The system used this information to create dynamic maintenance schedules.

4. **Integration with Maintenance Systems:** The predictive maintenance system was integrated with ArcelorMittal's maintenance management systems, allowing for the automatic scheduling of maintenance tasks when needed. This integration streamlined the process, reducing human intervention and ensuring that the right maintenance was performed at the right time.

Results and Benefits:

1. **Reduced Unplanned Downtime:** By predicting potential equipment failures before they occurred, ArcelorMittal was able to avoid many instances of unplanned downtime. The ability to address problems early allowed the company to perform maintenance when it was least disruptive to operations.

2. **Cost Savings on Maintenance:** Predictive maintenance helped ArcelorMittal reduce unnecessary preventive maintenance tasks that were based solely on time intervals, rather than actual equipment condition. This optimization resulted in cost savings related to spare parts, labor, and downtime. Furthermore, by avoiding sudden breakdowns, the company saved on emergency repair costs.

3. **Increased Equipment Lifespan:** The predictive maintenance system helped extend the life of critical

equipment. By monitoring equipment health and performing maintenance based on actual wear and tear, rather than fixed intervals, the company could ensure that machinery was running at optimal efficiency for longer periods.

4. **Improved Production Efficiency:** With fewer equipment failures, ArcelorMittal's production lines operated more smoothly and consistently, leading to better overall production efficiency. This also allowed for more predictable delivery schedules, which helped maintain customer satisfaction.

5. **Data-Driven Decision Making:** The AI-driven predictive maintenance system provided ArcelorMittal with valuable insights into the performance of its equipment. The company was able to make data-driven decisions regarding which machines required upgrades or replacement, enabling better long-term capital planning.

6. **Sustainability Benefits:** By optimizing maintenance schedules and extending the life of equipment, ArcelorMittal reduced its environmental impact. Fewer breakdowns meant less waste and more efficient use of resources, contributing to sustainability goals.

Conclusion: ArcelorMittal's implementation of AI-driven predictive maintenance exemplifies how artificial intelligence can transform operations in the steel industry. By combining IoT, machine learning, and advanced analytics, ArcelorMittal was able to significantly reduce unplanned downtime, lower maintenance costs, and improve overall equipment efficiency. This case study highlights the potential for AI to optimize maintenance in steel production plants, ultimately driving cost savings and enhancing production reliability in a highly complex manufacturing environment.

13.6 Case Study 6: AI-based Energy Optimization in Steel Production at Tata Steel

Introduction:

Tata Steel, one of the largest steel manufacturers globally, has leveraged artificial intelligence (AI) to enhance its steel production processes. One of the key areas where AI has been applied is in energy optimization within its manufacturing operations. The steel production process is highly energy-intensive, with significant energy requirements for melting, refining, and shaping steel. To reduce operational costs and environmental impact, Tata Steel implemented AI-powered solutions to optimize its energy consumption.

Challenge:

The steelmaking process involves the consumption of large amounts of energy, especially in electric arc furnaces (EAF) and blast furnaces. The challenge was to optimize energy usage, reduce waste, and lower operational costs while maintaining production efficiency and minimizing environmental impacts like CO_2 emissions. Traditional methods of energy management were either time-based or reactive, often leading to inefficient energy use. Tata Steel wanted to employ AI to predict and optimize energy consumption in real-time, thus improving both cost efficiency and sustainability.

AI Implementation:

Tata Steel implemented an AI-driven energy optimization system designed to monitor and manage energy consumption across its steel production facilities in real-time. The key components of this system included:

1. **Data Collection and Integration:** Sensors were deployed across various stages of the steel production process to collect real-time data on energy consumption, temperature, pressure, and other variables critical to the operation. This data was integrated into a centralized system for analysis.

2. **Machine Learning Algorithms:** Tata Steel employed machine learning (ML) algorithms to analyze the historical and real-time data. The algorithms were trained to detect patterns and correlations between energy consumption and various production parameters such as furnace temperature, raw material quality, and production speed. By understanding these patterns, the system could predict future energy requirements more accurately and suggest adjustments to optimize energy use.

3. **Real-time Energy Management:** The AI system continuously monitored energy consumption across different production units (including blast furnaces and rolling mills). By forecasting energy demand based on real-time data and predictive analytics, the system was able to adjust parameters such as furnace temperatures and load distribution in real-time to minimize energy consumption without compromising output quality.

4. **Optimization Recommendations:** The AI system provided actionable insights and optimization recommendations to plant operators. For example, it suggested changes to furnace operational settings or adjustments in the timing of various stages of production to align with optimal energy use patterns. These recommendations helped plant managers make data-driven decisions to reduce energy wastage.

5. **Energy Demand Forecasting:** AI models were used to forecast future energy demand based on historical trends, weather conditions, and other influencing factors. These forecasts allowed Tata Steel to plan energy procurement more efficiently, reducing reliance on peak-hour energy tariffs and lowering overall energy costs.

Results and Benefits:

1. **Reduced Energy Consumption:** By optimizing furnace operations and predicting energy needs more accurately, Tata Steel achieved a reduction in overall energy consumption. The AI system's ability to adjust operational parameters in real-time ensured that energy

was used more efficiently, particularly during high-energy demand phases of production.

2. **Cost Savings:** The optimization of energy consumption translated into significant cost savings. Tata Steel reduced its energy costs by minimizing waste and avoiding over-consumption during non-peak hours. The predictive nature of the AI system also enabled the company to better manage energy procurement, reducing its exposure to volatile energy prices.

3. **Environmental Benefits:** The energy optimization process contributed to a reduction in CO_2 emissions. By using energy more efficiently, Tata Steel was able to lower its carbon footprint, aligning with its sustainability goals. This was a significant achievement for a sector known for its high environmental impact.

4. **Enhanced Operational Efficiency:** The AI-powered energy optimization system improved the overall operational efficiency of Tata Steel's plants. The plant's equipment operated at optimal conditions, reducing the likelihood of breakdowns or inefficiencies caused by energy surges or fluctuations.

5. **Scalability and Future Impact:** Tata Steel's AI-powered energy optimization system proved to be scalable across its multiple production facilities, offering the potential for further expansion and improvements in other regions. The insights and efficiency gained through AI also provided the company with the ability to further innovate and apply similar strategies in other areas of production, such as water usage and waste management.

Conclusion:

Tata Steel's implementation of AI-driven energy optimization is an excellent example of how artificial intelligence can revolutionize energy management in the steel industry. By integrating real-time data collection, machine learning, and predictive analytics, Tata Steel was able to optimize energy consumption, reduce costs, improve efficiency, and contribute to environmental sustainability. This case study demonstrates the potential for AI to drive significant improvements in energy-intensive industries like steel production, setting a benchmark for other companies in the sector to follow.

13.7 Case Study 7: AI-driven Supply Chain Optimization in Steel Industry – ArcelorMittal

Introduction: ArcelorMittal, one of the world's largest steel manufacturing companies, has integrated artificial intelligence (AI) into its supply chain operations to enhance efficiency and reduce costs. The company implemented AI-driven supply chain optimization techniques to handle the complexities involved in sourcing, production, and distribution of steel products. By leveraging AI, ArcelorMittal sought to improve forecasting, reduce stockouts, optimize inventory levels, and minimize waste.

Challenge:

The steel industry's supply chain faces significant challenges, including fluctuating raw material prices, unpredictable demand, long lead times, and the complexity of coordinating global operations. ArcelorMittal's supply chain was fragmented, with multiple facilities, numerous suppliers, and vast geographic reach. This made it difficult to predict raw material demand accurately, maintain optimal inventory levels, and avoid production delays. Additionally, the company aimed to improve its logistics network to reduce transportation costs and enhance overall supply chain efficiency.

AI Implementation:

To address these challenges, ArcelorMittal implemented AI-powered solutions across various areas of its supply chain:

1. **Demand Forecasting and Inventory Optimization:** AI algorithms were applied to historical data to predict raw material demand more accurately. This allowed ArcelorMittal to forecast production requirements, manage raw material stock levels, and optimize inventory. By analyzing data from multiple sources (such as market trends, customer orders, and external factors like economic indicators), the system could predict fluctuations in demand and adjust inventory accordingly, reducing the risk of overstocking or stockouts.

2. **Supply Chain Network Optimization:** ArcelorMittal used AI to optimize the flow of raw materials through its global supply chain. Machine learning algorithms analyzed data from various plants, suppliers, and distribution centers to determine the most efficient routes and schedules for delivery. By optimizing routes for transporting raw materials to production facilities and finished products to customers, ArcelorMittal reduced transportation costs and lead times, improving the overall efficiency of its supply chain network.

3. **Supplier Performance Evaluation:** AI-driven analytics were used to assess supplier performance by analyzing factors such as delivery times, quality of materials, and consistency in supply. The system provided actionable insights that helped ArcelorMittal select the most reliable suppliers and reduce the risk of delays or quality issues in production. This supplier optimization further enhanced supply chain stability and reduced production disruptions.

4. **Predictive Analytics for Production Scheduling:** AI-powered predictive analytics were applied to forecast the best production schedules based on real-time demand data and available raw materials. By aligning production schedules with market demand, ArcelorMittal minimized production downtime and optimized factory utilization. This also allowed the company to better manage labor resources and reduce waste from overproduction or underproduction.

5. **Real-time Monitoring and Decision Support:** ArcelorMittal implemented AI-based decision support systems that provided real-time insights and recommendations for supply chain managers. This allowed for quick adjustments to be made in response to unexpected disruptions, such as raw material shortages or shipping delays. The system provided a dynamic, data-driven approach to supply chain management that could adapt to changing conditions.

Results and Benefits:

1. **Improved Forecast Accuracy:** AI-enhanced demand forecasting led to more accurate predictions of raw material needs. This helped ArcelorMittal optimize its inventory management, ensuring that the right amount of raw materials was available at the right time, without overstocking or stockouts. The company was able to reduce excess inventory costs while maintaining the ability to meet production demands.

2. **Cost Reduction:** Through better demand forecasting, transportation optimization, and inventory management, ArcelorMittal achieved significant cost reductions. The AI-driven system helped identify inefficiencies in the supply chain, leading to reduced transportation costs and minimized wastage in raw materials and finished goods.

3. **Faster Response to Market Changes:** The predictive capabilities of the AI system allowed ArcelorMittal to respond more quickly to shifts in market demand, such as fluctuations in steel prices or changes in customer requirements. This agility gave the company a competitive edge, as it could adjust its operations in near real-time to meet changing market conditions.

4. **Optimized Supply Chain Network:** AI allowed ArcelorMittal to streamline its logistics operations, cutting down transportation costs by optimizing delivery routes and schedules. This resulted in a more efficient use of resources and a reduction in CO_2 emissions associated with transportation.

5. **Enhanced Supplier Relationships:** The use of AI to evaluate supplier performance helped ArcelorMittal identify the most reliable suppliers and strengthen relationships with them. By ensuring consistent and high-quality supply, the company reduced risks associated with material shortages or delays, ensuring smoother production schedules.

6. **Sustainability and Efficiency:** The AI-driven optimizations reduced waste in both the raw material and production stages, contributing to the company's

sustainability goals. By optimizing resource use, ArcelorMittal was able to lower its carbon footprint, reduce material wastage, and align with industry sustainability standards.

Conclusion:

ArcelorMittal's AI-driven supply chain optimization is a prime example of how advanced technology can address the complexities of managing a global steel supply chain. By leveraging AI for demand forecasting, logistics optimization, and real-time decision support, ArcelorMittal significantly improved efficiency, reduced costs, and enhanced its competitive position in the market. This case study highlights the potential for AI to transform supply chain operations in the steel industry and underscores the importance of technology in achieving sustainability and operational excellence.

www.ingramcontent.com/pod-product-compliance
Lightning Source LLC
LaVergne TN
LVHW022335060326
832902LV00022B/4059